D1269853

The Lunacy Boom

Books by William Zinsser

Any Old Place with You

Seen Any Good Movies Lately?

The City Dwellers

Weekend Guests

The Haircurl Papers

Pop Goes America

The Paradise Bit (*novel*)

The Lunacy Boom

The Lunacy Boom

William Zinsser

HARPER & ROW, PUBLISHERS

NEW YORK, EVANSTON, AND LONDON

The material in this book originated in *Life* except "Perelman Revisited," *The New York Times Magazine;* "Peabody's Complaint" and "Doctor Dolittle," *The New York Times Book Review;* "The Right to Fail" and "Thank God for Nuts," *Look,* and "An Apple a Day Keeps the Flexowriter Away" and "Quenchless Me and Omphalocentric You," *Horizon.* I particularly want to thank Ralph Graves and David Scherman of *Life* for their encouragement and help.

W. Z.

 For information address Harper & Row, Publishers, Inc., 49 East 33rd Street, New York, N.Y. 10016. Published simultaneously in Canada by Fitzhenry & Whiteside Limited, Toronto.

FIRST EDITION

LIBRARY OF CONGRESS CATALOG CARD NUMBER: 74-127220

FOR CAROLINE
With Love

Contents

Introduction

I USED TO THINK that a hydrogen bomb explosion was the one sight that even the tireless American sightseer never wanted to see. But then I came upon an article in the travel and resort section of the *New York Times*—nestled among the Caribbean cruises and Riviera nights—which said that the Atomic Energy Commission had decided to let tourists observe large-scale nuclear tests at its new site two hundred miles north of Las Vegas.

Unfortunately, the article explained, "Observers will not experience the blinding flashes, awesome fireballs and deafening roars of the early above-ground tests. But even at a distance of twelve miles an underground megaton shot produces an artificial earthquake that makes the ground shudder and seemingly heave a couple of feet, a shock that can knock a man off his feet. A spectacular curtain of dust, miles wide, is sent up from the desert floor. There is always a possibility that the huge caverns blasted underground may cause a spectacular surface cave-in. The principal unexpected thing that can happen is a venting of radioactive gas through unpredictable fissures in the ground. . . ." And it went on to describe other sightseeing treats. I could only take it to mean that our nuclear arsenal has somehow crossed over from the realm of American defense to the realm of American leisure—a fun facility for Dad, Mom and the kids. Undecided about your vacation? Already done Disneyland? Why not go to Nevada for the blasts?

Of course I could hardly believe what I was reading. But this didn't surprise me—a central new fact of American life is that much of it is literally incredible. Am I really supposed to believe that atomic tests are now in the same recreation league as Old Faithful and Cypress Gardens? It's some kind of crazy joke.

But the crazy joke is that it's no joke. Today in America the outlandish becomes routine overnight, and after that nobody gives it a second thought.

This book represents a continuing attempt over the past few years—mainly in *Life*—to give it a second thought. Many pieces that I wrote then are not included here. They briefly froze some passing trend that melted again and moved on—trends no longer do us the favor of holding still for a decent amount of time. In fact, Andy Warhol says the day is near when people will be famous for fifteen minutes.

Typical of the instant obsolescence which gnaws at the edges of satire is the chapter called "Commencement Address," and I include it as a historic curio only two years old. It was written as a comment on the turmoil that was sweeping Columbia and other colleges in the spring of 1968. Campus revolt was then a new American phenomenon, and every day the papers reported some new seizure of a president's office or the spawning of a new ad hoc committee. Since then, of course, student protest has greatly deepened. Actual death on the campus and further death in Indochina have pushed it beyond local rhetoric and rioting to national political action, and now the mere capturing of a dean seems almost as frivolous as a panty raid.

Still, when "Commencement Address" appeared in *Life*, it was not only topical; it was even ahead of the events that it was lampooning. It ran in May, before any college had held its graduation, and it broached the absurd idea that dissident seniors might hold their own dissident commencements as a protest. A week later Columbia had its graduation and the dissidents did just that. The absurd became a reality.

Again, I wasn't surprised. The serious humorist gets nearer every day to the front lines of journalism. He is in a perpetual race with life; his home crackles with the sound of preposterous items being torn out of the newspaper. Sometimes he can pin down a particular lunacy long enough for the reader to see how lunatic it is, as Herblock and Bill Mauldin and Art Buchwald do remarkably often. But increasingly it is life that thinks up the gag that can't be topped, and then the humorist gives up in defeat. Last fall I clipped the following news story:

> DALLAS (AP)—The Muscular Dystrophy Assn. has called off the fund-raising gimmick it had planned here for Nov. 29.
>
> Teenage volunteers armed with toy guns were to have taken part in a "holdup for muscular dystrophy"—seeking contributions at Dallas shopping centers.
>
> Eight holdups of banking institutions since Sept. 22, two

> hotel clerk robbery-murders and assorted other gunplay have made Dallas too jittery even for toy guns, Bill Stone, associate representative, said yesterday.

Dallas, of all cities. November, of all months. Guns, of all gimmicks. You guys are too much.

Or consider this incident that took place at the White House last May when a group of Congressmen came to be briefed on the Cambodian "incursion" that had just been launched without their consent. Senator Claiborne Pell of Rhode Island said that it didn't sound like a limited action because it was named "Operation Total Victory." President Nixon replied that "I, as President, don't name the operations. It was the South Vietnamese who used the code name 'Total Victory.'" At this point Henry Kissinger, the President's adviser, slightly corrected the boss.

"Mr. President," he said, "the South Vietnamese give that term to all their operations. This happens to be Operation Total Victory Number 43."

No gagwriter could come up with a better gag. When Kissinger begins to sound like Woody Allen, it's later than we think.

So why even try to write humor against such competition? Only, if possible, to jolt the reader into seeing plainly what is plainly ludicrous in America at the start of the 1970s, to say: "Look, something crazy is going on here, some erosion in the quality of life, or some grave threat to life itself, and it's outlandish, and yet everybody accepts it as normal." The serious humorist is trying to point out that it really is still outlandish.

The Fair S-x

IT WAS JUST a simple accident—the pretty girl sitting next to me at dinner spilled something on her dress—and I wouldn't have noticed it except for her unusual reaction.

"G-d d--- it!" she yelled.

"Mercy me!" I said. "What's the matter?"

"How the h--- do they expect us to eat this cr-p?"

"Land sakes, who are you talking about?" I asked.

"Those sons of b-----s out in the kitchen," she snapped.

"Gracious, a thing like that could happen to any of us," I told her, and that seemed to calm her down. Still, the incident left me shaken and I didn't know what to make of it. Then I saw a headline in the *New York Times:*

WOMEN INFRINGING ON
ANOTHER MEN'S PREROGATIVE:
THE FREEDOM TO CURSE

"Tarnation!" I said to myself (for the headline really made me mad). "Will they never stop this blasted infringing!"

The article said that "the use of obscene language among women, from coeds of the New Left to proper matrons at swank Manhattan cocktail parties, has risen sharply. Police have been amazed by the obscenity issuing from the lips of apparently demure girls at political demonstrations."

But why would an apparently demure girl want to do a thing like that? One theory suggested that many women lost their inhibitions when "the beautiful people and female movie stars started doing it." The theory is all right as far as it goes (which isn't very far), but it has a flaw. For when the beautiful people started using foul language, didn't they become less beautiful people, or even somewhat ugly people? That's the trouble with having the beautiful people around as a new American class. Just when they're so beautiful it almost makes you want to cry, they turn around and do something gross, and then all our values go p--f.

So if it isn't a question of beauty, what is it a question of? Raw power, says a psychologist who taught at Columbia and found that Barnard girls were much more likely than Columbia men to "curse a cop" during the campus riots. "They were aware that cursing was a weapon, one of the few they had," the psychologist explained, and they used it for two revolutionary ends—to exploit class differences and thereby enrage the police, whose own women don't curse in public, and to establish equality with Columbia men.

Thus feminism finds its ultimate tool—the four-letter word—and drives for total victory. And who shall hurl it back, this Anglo-Saxon tide? I don't mind women having the vote, or holding male jobs, or going to men's colleges, or any of that Women's Liberation stuff. We will even survive their wearing men's suits. But the toughest cop won't withstand the obscenity of an apparently demure girl. Let him spray her with Mace; she will spray him back with expletives and he will crumble. So much for law and order.

And how can a husband come home at night to a family where he is not only outvoted but outsworn? This was one of his few areas of domestic competence—a rude skill, but at least his very own, the vestigial reward of his army years when he fought for his country while the little woman stayed home and made apple pie. Now the little woman stays home to read dirty novels and practice her vocabulary, and a husband who opens the door to announce that he had a heck of a hard day, or that he got a darn good raise, will find himself blown back out on the sidewalk, a victim of the new equality. So much for the American home.

Well, swear away, girls, if that will make you feel manly. But at least break some new ground. Surely it's no victory to use the same few tired words in which men have tried for so long to wrap their virility or to bury their frustrations. Invent! Be creative! Bring feminine grace and feminist intellect to profanity's arid shores.

If a cop gets too nosy, call him a dirty scrutator. If you see him stealing an apple, tell him he's full of usufruct. Accuse him of manumission at least once a day. Taunt your husband for being intestate. Complain that he drinks too much to labialize. Say you caught him fossicking in the attic, or animadverting on your best friend. Coeds, demand formication in the biology lab and rectorial rights on Sunday. Shout the new words with gusto at riots and rallies: sphagnum, flocculate, nuptials, surd! Fuscous, ropery, lingulate, ort! Scutum, pismire, fruticose, nard! They're all there in Webster's, hundreds of them, just waiting to be used. If you really want a weapon, ladies, *that's* how to knock the futtock out from under the ship of state.

[BLIP] Is Beautiful

GOOD EVENING. This is David Ruskin, host of tonight's Channel 15 symposium on "The New Permissiveness: Renaissance or Ruin?" Our guests are Wendy Mankowitz, star of the new hit musical *Skin!*, in which she performs fourteen simulated sexual acts, both natural and unnatural, beating the previous record of eleven set by Cerise Hagerty in the satirical nude revue *Mace;* Ronnie Plumb, the brilliant English impresario whose "evening of civilized voyeurism," *F*, is a Broadway sellout at $27.50 a seat; Ulu Sjønqvist, director of the Swedish film *I Am Virgin*, hailed by New York critics for its sensitive treatment of a young girl's discovery of herself through her bizarre love for a stallion, Sven; and the Reverend Enoch Moody, whose outspoken sermon in Yankee Stadium, "Whither the Protestant Ethic?," has made him the spokesman for clergymen and laymen alike seeking a viable answer to the sexual revolt which is shaking middle-class values to their very foundation. We're in for a fun evening, so let's get started with a question to Miss Mankowitz. Wendy, I notice you're not wearing anything tonight. Is that a conscious decision on your part—going nude on TV—or did you just forget to put on your clothes?

MISS MANKOWITZ: No, David, it's very definitely a conscious decision. My personal philosophy is that "bare is beautiful" and anyone who wears clothes has got to be some kind of creep.

PLUMB: Bravo, Miss Mankowitz—precisely the existential premise of my little show, *F*. If audiences can go to the theater and see people doing beautiful things to each other with no clothes on, they'll go home and—you know—get in the bathtub together instead of making war or making money. *F* is very definitely a political statement.

RUSKIN: You're saying, in other words, that it has redeeming social value?

PLUMB: Naturally, my dear chap. If one didn't feel that one were making some contribution to the human condition, one might feel that one was simply producing smut, wouldn't one?

MISS MANKOWITZ: Oh, you mustn't think that! Like I sometimes hear that audiences come to see me act in the nude because I just happen to have a beautiful pair of [BLIP]. What they don't understand is that I am interposing my naked body against the violence of Vietnam and Chicago and the whole military-industrial complex. Why, if Melvin Laird took off his clothes when he went into the Pentagon we'd have peace in two weeks.

RUSKIN: Isn't that the very point that you are trying to make, Mr. Sjønqvist, in your film *I Am Virgin?*

SJØNQVIST: Exactly: that we must cultivate an awareness of our essential innocence. The girl in my film, Sigrid, symbolizes Truth; the stallion, Sven, represents the Establishment, and in the scene where she undresses and they [BLIP] in the meadow outside the summer palace of King Ulric, I am obviously making a deeply felt point about unilateral disarmament.

MOODY: And that's what people are coming to see? I hear the box-office line is two blocks long. You're not just pandering to their prurient appetites?

SJØNQVIST: Never! Every person who goes to *I Am Virgin* is motivated by a sincere need to fantasize through this allegorical psychodrama his fear of brute technocracy overpowering the individual in an increasingly impersonal society. It never occurred to me that audiences would find my film erotic. The girl isn't even that sexy—did you think so, David?

RUSKIN: Well, she has pretty good [BLIP] but she's kind of chubby around the [BLIP].

SJØNQVIST: Right! It's those two or three inches of extra fat that give the film its artistic integrity. You know from the first time you see the girl—that scene in the shower—that *I Am Virgin* is an intellectual exercise.

MOODY: It's pornography.

PLUMB: Come, come, Reverend—you know there's no such thing as pornography in America any more. The very concept is an outmoded relic of Victorian prudery perpetuated by guys like you with a Judeo-Christian ethics hang-up.

MOODY: But surely the law recognizes a distinction between what is obscene and what is—

PLUMB: It did until last week, when Judge Wagenseller overturned the obscenity conviction of the publisher of *Phallic Weekly*. There are no more guidelines.

RUSKIN: He's a beautiful human being, Judge Wagenseller.

MOODY: He's an idiot! Why, I'm told that the photographs in that magazine were nothing but couples engaged in—how shall I put it?

PLUMB: [BLIP BLIP] and [BLIP] and also some [BLIP].

MOODY: Yes. Quite. And aren't such pictures considered pornography?

PLUMB: Judge Wagenseller ruled that the photographs were basically educational and were therefore protected under the Constitutional guarantees of freedom of information.

MOODY: Well, there's still the law of God. Vengeance is mine, saith the Lord. Mark my words: a civilization which is reduced to getting cheap kicks is a civilization in decay!

MISS MANKOWITZ: I think God wants me to go naked. I feel He's telling me that the vulnerability of my body is a meaningful answer to the hypocrisy and materialism of the times we live in.

RUSKIN: You think God digs you—right?

MISS MANKOWITZ: He's groovy. Say, aren't you hot under these lights, David? Why don't you take off your clothes?

RUSKIN: Beautiful. . . . There, that feels better. Anybody else? Gosh, Ronnie, you sure get out of that turtleneck fast. You too, Mr. Sjønqvist—hey, that's a crazy place for a tattoo. Wild, man! That just leaves you, Reverend. You look mighty uptight in that clerical collar. How about it?

MOODY: Oh, heavens. Why not?

Come Back, Nipper!
Where Are You, Chessie?

I KEEP LOSING American companies. Every week two or three more disappear, taking with them their name, their trademark, and my memories. It makes me nervous. Suddenly everybody is GAF or GAC or GCA. Or Dayco or Citgo or Armco. Or National General. National General *what?* Two adjectives and no noun. I miss the noun. I no longer know what business American businesses are in.

Remember Pittsburgh Plate Glass, the company that made plate glass in Pittsburgh? Now it's PPG Industries, presumably making ppg's. Where have you gone, Corn Products? I used to like to think of you making corn products. Now you're CPC International—unless that's somebody else—and I don't think of you at all. Or of any other company that took some commodity out of my life by burrowing into the alphabet. Mining went out of the

3M Company, and so did manufacturing and Minnesota; the shoe machinery went out of USM, the rubber out of Uniroyal. What can a man hang on to?

Is the Minneapolis & St. Paul Railway really MSL Industries, Inc.? Or the Alaska Juneau Gold Mining Company really A. J. Industries, Inc.? Say it ain't so! Did railroaders push west and prospectors push north to die in a desert of initials? Did founders found business to serve real needs that would be smothered in fake names? Take the American Molasses Company. I doubt if there's a man or boy who doesn't like to picture a company that's sitting around all day making molasses. Well, that picture's over. The firm vanished, and when I found it again it was SuCrest. What's SuCrest to me, or me to SuCrest?

I don't even insist on knowing exactly what a company does. All I ask is a decent clue. I've never understood, for instance, how the Air Reduction Company makes any money reducing air, but that's evidently what it does, and I think of it with fondness. Not so the Automatic Sprinkler Corporation of America, which I'm quite sure made automatic sprinklers. Now it's A-T-O. And I'm Apathy Industries, Inc.

I first began to notice the loss of business identity and all the emotional baggage that goes with it—a sense of American history and growth and regional flavor—a few years ago when RCA banished Nipper, its trademark dog, and I wondered if Nipper was the only animal to get the corporate boot. Elsie the cow was still safe inside her daisy on Borden's milk-based products. But where was Chessie, the cat who used to sleep so peacefully on the Chesapeake & Ohio's Pullman trains? She always made me partial to the C & O. Not that I wanted a cat in my berth, but the company seemed to be a friendly one.

Now Chessie has all but disappeared, and my affection has lapsed. And where did that Flying Red Horse go? Amid such extinction I'm grateful to the Mack bulldog and the Greyhound greyhound and the few human symbols who haven't been killed off, like Psyche, the White Rock girl, still perched on her rock in America's original minidress. They are relics of individuality in an age when everything suddenly looks alike.

Even Metropolitan Life's beacon, "The Light That Never Fails," failed. The bulb went out and it has been replaced by a logotype of eight geometric points. John Hancock's signature has largely yielded to a JOHN HANCOCK printed as John himself never printed it, and the Bell System's bell has been progressively streamlined so that it now looks like a Nazi helmet.

RCA's Nipper, of course, never had a chance of lasting into the 1970s, and his case is a perfect example of the whole phenomenon. Nipper had been sitting pensively in front of an old record player, his head almost inside the speaker, since RCA was a pup, and anybody who liked dogs couldn't help liking the Radio Corporation of America, as it was then called. But meanwhile RCA grew far beyond radios and beyond America. Today it makes twelve thousand products, including computers, and I can see why it would want an image more sophisticated than a fox terrier mooning into the horn of a wind-up Victrola.

So out went the graceful old monogram—three letters in a circle, with a bolt of lightning streaking out of the *A*—and in came an RCA so aggressively modern that one of the house computers might have designed it. And out went Nipper except on one product, Red Seal Records, which cater to nostalgia by preserving great singers of the past, and there he sits, still listening to "His Master's Voice," still appreciated. The Caruso crowd isn't the computer crowd, and at least Nipper will never be in *that* doghouse.

But otherwise RCA has chosen to ride into the future without him, secure in having three well-known letters to cover an infinite variety of products—the envy, like IBM, of countless firms that have recently merged or diversified and are now struggling to create a new identity that the public will, if not love, at least recognize. Their efforts have had some odd results.

When Life Savers merged with Beech-Nut it became Beech-Nut Life Savers, which hardly sounded appetizing. Then it merged with E. R. Squibb & Sons to become Squibb Beech-Nut, which sounded even worse, and Life Savers disappeared altogether. So did Squibb's sons. As a Life Saver addict I miss my company, just as I'm sure cigar and drugstore fans felt a sense of loss when United Cigars and Whelan Stores became the United Whelan Corp. What are whelans anyway, and why do they need to be united?

But I should know better than to look for sense—or sentiment—in American business any more. Buying other companies to form a giant conglomerate is now, as they say in Wall Street, the name of the game. But what's the name of the giant conglomerate? TRX. GATX. AVCO. ELTRA. Forget it. And who won't? Today big businesses own so many other big businesses that one product name can no longer tell their story. Even Hershey Chocolate had to change into Hershey Foods Corp. last year because it bought several companies that don't—(SOB!)—make candy. One-third of its sales, in fact, now come from such foods as macaroni, and I'll never feel quite the same driving through Hershey, Pa., "the town that chocolate built," especially at the intersection where Chocolate

Avenue meets Cocoa Street. In another ten years it will be Lasagna Avenue and Minestrone Street.

I noticed the other day that the Heinz logotype no longer says "57 Varieties." Obviously the company has diversified and now makes a thousand and fifty-seven varieties—of what I can't even imagine. Probably the firm is up to its neck in aerospace. All I'm sure of is that one more slogan has slipped out of our lives, and my children don't know what in tarnation their grandfather is talking about when he says, "That man has more troubles than Heinz has pickles."

A Slight Case of Ecology

CINCINNATI, April 1—The National Refractory & Brake Company announced plans today for construction of a $12,000,000 plant for the manufacture of low-density orthoxylene refrigerants and methylated polyresins at a 120-acre site fronting on the historic Cahoga River in southeastern Ohio, adjacent to the famed Frank J. Fenster Memorial Bird & Wildlife Preserve.

Extensive feasibility studies preceded selection of the site, according to Harley G. Waller, president of the giant petrochemical and software firm. "We looked into all the locational factors, especially with respect to stream hydrology and thermal inputs," he said, "and we're convinced that dollar for dollar the Ohio facility will give our stockholders optimal return."

Mr. Waller frankly noted the proximity of the new

plant to the Fenster nature preserve. However, he said, "you can be sure that N.R. & B. will not be unmindful of its responsibility to minimize through the utilization of electrostatic precipitators the discharge of effluents into the Cahoga and the per-hour ratio of air-pollution emissions, notably fly-ash particulates."

"I have every confidence that nature and industry can live harmoniously together in this beautiful valley," he added. "After all, I'm a country boy myself," he smiled.

DENVER, April 2—The Outdoor Society strongly protested today the decision of the National Refractory & Brake Company to build a new orthoxylene facility on a 120-acre site adjoining the Frank J. Fenster Bird & Wildlife Preserve. "I'm shocked, frankly," said Waldo B. Ott, president of the 21,000-member conservationist group, which spearheaded the recent lobby that was credited with blocking the installation by United Styrenic Corp. of an underground flotation mill in Yellowstone Park for the extraction of organic sulfonates.

"The siting of the National Refractory plant shows callous disregard for the ecological balance of the Cahoga River Basin and of the very biosphere," Mr. Ott charged in a press conference today. "The low-density orthoxylene process involves the release of gases which adversely affect the nasal membranes of all living creatures within a radius of 180 miles. Or, in laymen's terms, they stink. To emit these contaminants within the same climatological grid as the Fenster preserve, which is the known nesting ground of 78 bird species, including the threatened godwit, would be nothing less than a criminal assault on one of the last natural resources in the Allegheny ecosystem."

CINCINNATI, April 3—Dismissing the Outdoor Society as "just a bunch of bird nuts," Harley G. Waller, president of the National Refractory & Brake Company, lashed back today at the old and respected conservation group for its attempt to mobilize public opinion against construction of an orthoxylene facility adjacent to the Fenster Preserve.

"Frankly, I'm darn annoyed," Mr. Waller told reporters. "You can't turn a shovel in this country today without digging up a lot of birders and hikers. If all these nature kooks had their way, America would still be a wilderness from coast to coast. Thank God there are at least a few businessmen who care about the Gross National Product and don't get hung up on a couple of lousy godwits."

The News-Chronicle
April 4, 1970
FOR SHAME, MR. WALLER!

This newspaper has long upheld in its editorial columns the principle of free enterprise. That the capitalistic system is a cornerstone of America there can be no argument among all who have the vigorous growth of our nation at heart.

Yet the cause of enlightened business leadership is rendered a grave disservice by intemperate remarks of the type made yesterday by Mr. Harley G. Waller, president of the National Refractory & Brake Company, who crudely brushed off as "bird nuts" and "nature kooks" the conservationists who view with alarm—quite properly, it seems to us—the threat to the Fenster preserve posed by N.R. & B.'s plan for an orthoxylene facility on an adjacent tract. Surely the firm could have shown far more sensitivity in its choice of an industrial site, and Mr. Waller's comments to the press betray a woefully deficient grasp of good environmental and riparian planning—not to mention good public relations.

So clean up your language, Mr. Waller, if you really care about clean air. There are a lot of us bird nuts and nature kooks out here—and mighty proud of it!

INTER-OFFICE MEMO

FROM: Harley G. Waller

TO: George F. L. Magruder

George: Get these damn editorial writers and bird nuts off my neck.

H.G.W.

CINCINNATI, April 6—George F. L. Magruder, vice-president for public relations of the National Refractory & Brake Company, characterized as "a harmless little joke that unfortunately didn't quite come off" the remark of N.R. & B. boss Harley G. Waller about "bird nuts" and "nature kooks" that caused widespread editorial criticism across the United States yesterday.

Referring to Mr. Waller as "an irrepressible wag," Mr. Magruder described the Refractory chief as "an ardent troll fisherman and man-about-the-yard" who enjoys relaxing on weekends by mulching the hydrangeas that he grows with his wife, Marjorie, and their two children, Harley, Jr., and Heather-Sue. "I happen to know that he keeps 'Walden' on his bedside table and is particularly concerned about the plight of the curlew and the avocet in the Cahoga River basin."

Turning to "the more serious matter" of pollution safeguards at the new site, Mr. Magruder released the following statement:

"The National Refractory & Brake Company takes as its credo that a clean America is a good America. We have in consequence made it a point to familiarize ourselves with the Air and Water Quality Act, the Environmental Quality Act, and the Solid Waste Act.

"Accordingly, N.R. & B. engineers are now engaged in the systematic study of air-sampling data and pollution-abatement research, particularly with respect to the aeration of sewage sludge and the recycling of non-durables into the breeder reactor circuit and taking cognizance of the proposed Federal legislation to limit the per-pound addition of biochemical oxygen demand (BOD) to America's waterways. Exhaustive benefit-cost analysis presently indicates a not inconsiderable possibility of utilizing cyclonic collectors and geothermal or tidal power in the complex fractionation process currently projected for our orthoxylene and polyresin facility, with a consequent desulphurization hopefully of the surrounding ecostructure and an attendant reduction of SO_2 emissions.

"Personally I am very grateful," Mr. Magruder added, "for this opportunity to make our position perfectly clear."

INTER-OFFICE MEMO
FROM: Harley G. Waller
TO: George F. L. Magruder
What the hell is "Walden"?

H.G.W.

ZANESVILLE, April 8—Two dozen members of Students Organized for Radical Ecology (SORE) staged a "dump-in" yesterday at the regional office of the National Refractory & Brake Company in downtown Zanesville. Arriving by electric truck from nearby Medford College, they deposited what police described as "a large quantity" of used beer cans and non-returnable soft-drink bottles at the main entrance of the building.

"We were making a symbolic protest," explained Mike Bottomley, bearded 20-year-old junior, "against the verbal garbage of vice-president Magruder's statement to the press. We think that one load of garbage deserves another, and we will continue to dump rotten junk on the rotten Establishment until the whole rotten society blows up."

Young Bottomley spoke to reporters from his cell at Muskingum County Jail, where he was booked on charges of committing a visual nuisance.

WASHINGTON, April 9—The Justice Department announced today that it would begin the systematic fingerprinting, photographing and urinalysis of "all persons connected with the forces of conservation and environmental protection."

Attorney General John N. Mitchell said that "the violent incident of dumping on the property of a great American corporation proves that the conservation movement is a breeding ground of communists and other subversives. We intend to clean them out, even if it means rounding up every bird-watcher in the country."

Mr. Mitchell labeled it "unfortunate" that "many innocent people would have to be investigated just because of the action of a handful of young punks."

"But," he pointed out, "that's democracy."

MARIETTA, April 10—The ad hoc Citizens Committee for the Cahoga River Basin condemned as "wrongheaded" the dump-in held Tuesday by radical students from Medford College, which, it warned, could split the anti-pollution movement into activist, liberal, progressive and moderate camps.

"We've got to get together on our ecotactics," committee secretary Mason L. Purdy told reporters at an "ornithological teach-in" yesterday in Fenster Preserve. Mr. Purdy said he was in regular contact with 150 organizations, including the Audubon Society, the Sierra Club, the Nature Conservancy, the Wilderness Society, the John Muir Institute, the Izaak Walton League, Friends of the Earth, and the Citizens League Against the Sonic Boom, which are "dedicated to the prevention of ecological disaster by the non-violent spread of information."

"If those kids had to have their dump-in," Mr. Purdy said, "I personally wish they had dumped some litter that was educational, like bio-degradable beer cans, which are made to hold together on the grocer's shelf but succumb to bacteriological decay later. That way the kids could have made a mess and also made a point."

CLEVELAND, April 11—Formation of the Save-the-Godwit League was announced today by Mrs. Charlene Spooner, executive secretary. "We must not wake up one day to find this noble bird gasping for the very breath of life in a miasma of commercial soot," Mrs. Spooner asserted. "Surely the oil-soaked birds of Santa Barbara are trying to say something to us across this great country of ours. I submit that what they are trying to say is 'Save the godwit!' "

TO THE EDITOR OF THE NEWS-CHRONICLE:

As a grocer I was tremendously interested in your article on bio-degradable beer cans, for my wife and I have tried to stock both beer and soft drinks in these experimental containers, which we sincerely believe are the eventual answer in a "throwaway society" to the problem of solid-waste control now afflicting America's parks and other recreation areas.

I say "eventual" because it has been our experience that the manufacturing process remains to be perfected. Perhaps it is because our turnover is somewhat slow, but we have noticed frequent instances of cans succumbing to bacteriological decay while still "on the grocer's shelf." This presents definite problems in keeping the store dry and neat-appearing.

Very truly yours,
ROY B. ATTERBURY
"Roy & Lil's"
April 12

COLUMBUS, April 13—Friends of the Curlew, Citizens Against Extinction of the Eared Grebe, and the American Widgeon Society, at an unusual joint press conference today, angrily accused the Save-the-Godwit League of trying to "splinter" the ornithological conservation front. "They act as if their godwit was the only thing worth saving in the whole swamp," said F. Ray Burnett, spokesman for the three groups. "Candidly, we don't think it's that great a bird."

WASHINGTON, April 13—The Army Corps of Engineers gave its unqualified approval today to the construction of an orthoxylene facility on the banks of the Cahoga River by the National Refractory & Brake Company. "It dovetails nicely," said Col. Melvin Applegate, "with a project that we had intended to announce next week for filling in the Pontiac Marsh farther downstream to make a marina."

"Personally, I don't like a river that's too quiet," Col. Applegate said. "With any kind of planning, the Cahoga could be a 100-mile turnpike for power boats and a boon to your average recreationist. We'll want to give every assistance to National Refractory in damming the river at the factory site to create a sophisticated storage lagoon. This would markedly optimize the dilution of effluents discharged from the factory at periods when the water level would not otherwise be sufficiently high to provide tertiary or even secondary treatment of outpiped ambient residuals. Quite simply, it's just a matter of inducing augmentation of your low stream flow. We could do the whole thing with a bulldozer in about three weeks."

WASHINGTON, April 14—Perhaps the most dramatic protest yet mounted by the militant ecology movement took place shortly after midnight yesterday when the Washington municipal sewage system was diverted to flow into the parking lot and adjoining premises of the Corps of Engineers headquarters building at 1400 F Street.

The name "Applegate" was found scrawled in excrement on the main door. Police theorized that this was a reference to Col. Melvin Applegate, who warmly endorsed on Monday the construction of an orthoxylene facility adjacent to the Cahoga River and a dam to provide augmented water reserves for the treatment of discharged effluents.

The flow of raw sewage was not detected until approximately 4 A.M. when residents called police to complain of "an unusual odor."

Three Washington newspapers reported receiving the following telegram earlier in the day:

PIG ANTI-LIFE LACKEYS OF MILITARY-INDUSTRIAL RAPISTS MAKING $$$ FOR DEATH-OBSESSED AMERIKA THRU IMPERIALIST GENOCIDE RACIST EXPLOITATION OF THIRD-WORLD MINORITIES COUNTER-HUMAN DESTRUCTION OF ENVIRONMENT MUST DIE IN REVOLUTION OF RISING MUCK STOP YOU ARE WARNED STOP

TASK FORCE 6

Inspector T. B. McGraw of the decontamination squad refused to comment on a rumor that the militants were from the Weathermen chapter of Counter Revolution Against Polluters (CRAP) at nearby Branstead Technical College.

"I'll say this," Inspector McGraw ventured. "Whoever they were, they knew a lot about plumbing."

DENVER, April 15—The Outdoor Society called on the Nixon Administration today to repudiate "the bulldozer philosophy of government" which, it said, "permits the Corps of Engineers, the Transportation Department, the jetport builders, the strip miners and the oil drillers to plow up, pave and poison the American landscape without regard for the quality of American life."

Waldo B. Ott, president of the 21,000-member conservation group, minced no words in his appeal to the White House. "I'll mince no words," Mr. Ott said. "The Government is the biggest polluter of all. We call on President Nixon to prove the sincerity of his expressed interest in the environment by keeping the Corps of Engineers and the National Refractory & Brake Company out of the beautiful Cahoga Valley, which is such a priceless part of the heritage that we will bequeath to our children and our children's children." He reminded the President that the Fenster Preserve is "a known nesting place of the threatened godwit."

WASHINGTON, April 16—White House press secretary Ron Ziegler told reporters today that he felt that President Nixon felt that "there was something to be said for both sides" in the Cahoga Valley controversy. He said that he felt that the President felt that he ought to "look into all sides of the situation very carefully." Mr. Ziegler said that he felt that it was Mr. Nixon's feeling that "you have to move slowly on these things."

From 39102 to 36601,
From 38101 to 64502,
Wherever the Four Winds Blow . . .

THE GENERAL ACCOUNTING OFFICE, a branch of the government that presumably does our general accounting, has proposed that the town name be dropped from all our postmarks, leaving only the zip code to show where a letter came from. This would make it easier, according to Comptroller General Elmer B. Staats, to consolidate America's 33,000 small and scattered post offices, which, he says, are inefficient and "based on a nineteenth-century concept."

Thus Mr. Staats, whose own name is shockingly wasteful of the letter *a,* seems to be pointing us toward a total zip code age. Next we will be told to omit the town name when we *address* our letters—why clutter up the envelope with a lot of nineteenth-century history?—and from there it's only a jump to abolishing these names altogether.

What a day that will be for families who like to keep in touch efficiently:

Dear Mom and Dad:

Susan and I and the kids just got back to 10028 last night and found your nice letter telling us about your vacation in 33733. Do they really play all that shuffleboard in 33733? We've always liked the east coast of Florida better—you can't beat 33140 for good old sunshine. Or 33404.

We had a great drive across the country. Went to 14303 on Thursday to see the Falls, even though it *wasn't* our honeymoon, and then came down to 14202 for the night. Remember the old song, *Shuffle Off to 14202?* Friday we drove back by way of 13326 because Timmy wanted to see the Baseball Hall of Fame (and so did I). It's a pretty little town, 13326—I think you'd like it.

This meant we didn't get as far south as Colonial 23185, which was hard on Susan because you know how she loves antiques. I guess we'll have to do that in the spring when we go to 20013 to see the cherry blossoms. The girls felt that Timmy was getting all the breaks because we happened to drive through Wisconsin on a Sunday when the 54305 Packers had a home game. They were playing 75221 and I managed to get two tickets, so the girls had to go to a movie. It was *Gone with the Wind.* Susan has seen it about eighteen times, but she always gets a kick out of the burning of 30301.

I know it sounds trite, but there's nothing like "seeing America first" to give the kids a feeling for their heritage. They loved 63401, of course, because Mark Twain spent his boyhood there and it's right on the Mississippi, but I think they liked 62706 even better. Who wouldn't be excited by all that early Lincoln stuff? And of course we saw all the "tourist" sights. We spent a night in 86001 so we could go to the Grand Canyon the next day—didn't your friends the Potters used to live in 86001?—and from there we drove to 83001 so we'd be near the Grand Tetons. It really gave Timmy and Pam a feeling for the distances in this country. I mean, who'd think it was more than 700 miles from 86001 to 83001?

Another thing we enjoyed was how the song titles came flooding back when we saw the different road signs and studied the maps—songs like *Meet Me in 63178 Louie* and *37402 Choo-Choo*. Speaking of 37402, do you remember George and Buffy Watkins who used to live there? They've moved to 74103, which I remember is one of your favorite cities. Or am I thinking of 85702? Susan says I'm losing my memory—she notices it whenever we take a drive, and then she starts going on about how she misses the picturesque old place names like Albuquerque and Oskaloosa and Pocatello Falls. She loves names like that. Silly kid.

But I'll admit I made a real goof one morning when we set out and she told me it was 414 miles to 82212—her plan was to reach Jim and Peggy Thurlow's house by nightfall —and I thought she said it was 212 miles to 82414, which of course is where the Mooneys live, and you know we've talked about visiting the Mooneys ever since they got back from 96763, so I turned left instead of right, and I was taking it kind of slow because 212 miles is nothing at all, and by the time Susan got us turned around it was too late and we wound up in a motel in 82601 and never saw the Thurlows *or* the Mooneys, which was too bad, because heaven knows when we'll ever get out to the 80000s again. This country sure has a lot of small and scattered towns. Too bad some of them can't be consolidated.

Anyway, it's good to be back in 10028, polluted air and all. 10000 or 90000, home is best, I always say.

Love,

053–24–3272

Look, No Earthquake!

ALEUTIAN H-BOMB IS FIRED
WITHOUT SETTING OFF QUAKE
—Headline in the *New York Times*

How comforting it was to be told the good news right away, and right on page 1: our country hadn't caused an earthquake after all, or a tidal wave, with its megaton nuclear blast on the island of Amchitka. The newspapers obviously realized that this was the only thing that we readers really wanted to know. We never had any doubt that the bomb itself would go off—the Atomic Energy Commission has exploded 180 in Nevada since 1963, which is enough to get the hang of it.

What we did have some doubts about was whether the AEC could detonate the equivalent of 1.2 million tons of TNT, underground, on an island that lies squarely across the belt of seismic activity in the Pacific, without giving the earth more of a rumble than it bargained for. Any schoolboy knows that this area doesn't rest on the firmest of foundations. Hawaii alone has been hit by 85 tidal waves in the last 156 years, the most severe being one in 1946 that killed 143 people, destroyed 488 homes, and did $26 million worth of damage. Interestingly—if you like interesting facts—it was caused by an earthquake in the Aleutian Islands. Yet Hawaii has had it relatively easy; in Japan the destruction from tidal waves has been even worse. Ask any Japanese schoolboy.

And yet the test went all right! Look, no earthquake! There was a sigh of relief in the headlines, almost a tinge of surprise, and the articles themselves sped to the wonderful fact that nothing had gone seriously wrong. "You thought we'd goof it, but we didn't," the government seemed to be telling its citizens, especially the spoilsport conservationists and legislators who had worried that the blast might contaminate nature, animal life and relations with nearby countries. There are better ways to make friends with Russia, after all, than to give it a tidal wave.

But you worried over nothing, the government said. There was no escape of radioactivity (as far as we know). There was no upset of the ecological balance (we don't think). There were no sea species permanently affected (we've found that otter can take 300 lbs. of overpressure). True, there did appear to be "some slippage" of the earth (but in this business you've got to expect a little slippage). In short, we're convinced that it's O.K. to go ahead now and set off two *really* big blasts, maybe 5 megatons (we've got to test those ABM nuclear warheads *some*where, and you know darn well that if we go much above a megaton in Nevada we shake the high-rise buildings in Las Vegas). Besides, we've spent $125 million just digging these three holes (it would be a shame not to use them). Anyway, it will be perfectly safe (we're quite sure).

So America enters a new age, the era of "thank God" journalism, its headlines specially written to tell us that a possible disaster didn't happen and that Providence has safely brought us to the beginning of another day. It's not much of a diet: solace for blunder unblundered. But we're going to see a lot more of it in the years ahead—if there are any years ahead—as complacent men tinker with the odds of survival. I would rather have our newspapers nourish us with positive feats and worthier goals. But perhaps Aquarius is over and we have slipped into the sign of Amchitka, where negative victories and near misses are the best that we will get—or deserve.

The otter isn't alone, after all, in being subjected to overpressure. The only difference is that the rest of us aren't being tested to see how much we can stand. In the case of the otter this was fairly easy to do—except for the animals that were having it done. They were placed in a pen just off Amchitka, as close to "ground zero" as possible, before the blast went off. The AEC admitted that a few might be killed—"pregnant females and pups are most susceptible"—but probably not many, because it had already run an otter test, bombarding them in a sealed tank of water with shock waves created by cannon shells. That's where it learned about the overpressure.

But what about us other species? What agency will test how much overpressure the American family can stand of crowding in the ghetto (pregnant females and pups are most susceptible), noise in the environment, pollution in the air, deprivation in the schools, inflation in the checkbook? Will anybody run a shock-wave test on the populace to determine which tolerable levels are really intolerable? Evidently not. It's easier to govern Amchitka-style—push the strains to the snapping point and then report the good news when nothing snaps:

TAXES UPPED TO 50 PERCENT
WITHOUT SETTING OFF RIOT

URBAN NOISE REACHES
HUMAN PAIN THRESHOLD
BUT NOBODY FREAKS OUT

"LETHAL" SMOG HITS EAST;
DEATH RISE ONLY "SLIGHT"

One of these days, of course, something will snap. After the Aleutian H-blast, for instance, one magazine reported that Amchitka "apparently survived intact." The island, in other words, is still there. Maybe next time it won't be. That's the beautiful suspense part. We'll never know until we try.

Humming a Different Tune

I LOVE THAT MOMENT every month when the statement arrives from the bank, or the bill from the gas and electric company, and out flutters a tiny leaflet telling me how lucky I am to be their customer. Nowhere does corporate boasting flower more profusely than in these enclosures, and over the years I've collected some wonderful specimens. They're sending me cleaner gas! They're giving me quieter current! They're processing my checks faster! Sometimes the people at the bank enclose a little packet of seeds so that I can plant petunias around the home that they want me to improve with their friendly 8¾% home improvement loan. I treasure the petunias because at that rate of interest they will constitute the only improving that gets done.

But the other day I bagged my finest trophy, a notice

that came enclosed with my bill from the New York Telephone Company. "Dear Customer," it said. "We'll be 'humming a different tune' when you pick up your telephone to make a call. You will hear a new dial tone—lower in pitch—which is the first step in a program to provide new equipment that will improve communications services. Others who use your telephone also might appreciate knowing the reason for the new dial tone."

Well, frankly, that part of it just hadn't occurred to me, and I was grateful to the firm for bringing it up. "Hey, Honey," I called to my wife, whose name happens to be Honey. "Did you know that the phone company is going to be 'humming a different tune' when you pick up your telephone to make a call? You will hear a new dial tone that's lower in pitch."

"Gosh, Dear," she said (my name happens to be Dear), "I wonder why they're doing that."

"It's the first step in a program to provide new equipment that will improve communications services."

"Why, that's fascinating," she said. "I certainly appreciate knowing it. And I think others who use our telephone also might appreciate knowing the reason for the new dial tone."

"You mean, you think we should tell the children?"

"Definitely," she said. "I wouldn't want them to pick it up in the street—they could get all sorts of misconceptions."

"You're so wise," I said, patting her hand, which happens to be at the end of her arm. "Other parents would keep it bottled up. But the kids are bound to find out anyway, and then they'd worry about it and would be too embarrassed to ask their mother or father."

I called in Sis and Junior (our kids happen to be named Sis and Junior) and told them about the new dial tone as frankly and openly as I could. I didn't try to cover up anything.

"Oh, Dad!" they both cried (they call me Dad). "Can we tell the baby-sitter when she comes tonight? She uses our telephone and might appreciate knowing."

"Sure," I said. "Tell anybody at all."

"You mean we can go next door and tell the Nelsons? And Pammy and Bob across the street? I'll bet anything they haven't heard about it yet."

I nodded, and they went racing out the door. Watching them, I felt warm all over.

"Dear," my wife said when they had gone, and I could tell that something was troubling her. "I wonder what the new dial tone will sound like."

"Do you want to hear it?"

"Oh, do you think we *could?*" she asked.

I picked up the telephone company's little printed notice and read aloud its last sentence, which I had been saving for just this moment. It said: "You may hear a recording of the new dial tone by dialing 734-1010."

Her eyes filled with tears. "You mean they went to all the bother of setting up a special number just so we could hear the new dial tone? Oh, isn't America a wonderful country!"

Well, that shot the weekend. First I dialed 734-1010 (I was first because I'm "head of the house") and listened to the new dial tone. It really sounded good, but I didn't want to hog the phone, so after a few minutes I hung up. "Your turn, Honey," I said. "Just dial 734-1010."

She did, and you never saw anyone so happy. In fact, when Sis and Junior came back they could hardly get the phone away from her. And of course I wanted another turn too.

"I like it *so* much better than the old dial tone," my wife purred.

"That lower pitch really grabs me," I agreed. "It must be around A-flat, and the other one was way the heck up around C, maybe even D."

"And isn't it a nice recording?" said Sis, who owns a lot of nice recordings.

"I hated the old dial tone," Junior blurted out, "but I didn't say anything because—you know—what good would it do? I never figured the telephone company would provide new equipment as groovy as this. Man, what an improvement in communications services!"

Just then the baby-sitter arrived and the kids hopped up and down with excitement when they went to open the door.

"Hey, Karen, you'll never guess!" Sis practically screamed at her.

"It's a new dial tone! Lower in pitch!" Junior chimed in.

"Come on, you've just got to listen to it," they both cried, pulling her over to the phone. The poor girl didn't even have time to take off her coat.

We hated it that we had to leave, but at least we knew that Karen and the kids were set for a fun evening and wouldn't waste it watching TV. Luckily, the next day was Saturday, so we had plenty of free time, and around noon we asked some neighbors in to listen to the new dial tone with us. We made a big point of telling them what the company's purpose was in making the change because we could see from their faces that the question was nagging them: "Why? Why did the telephone company do it?" They really appreciated knowing the reason.

Block That Chickenfurter

I'VE OFTEN wondered what goes into a hot dog. Now I know and I wish I didn't.

It all started when the Department of Agriculture published the hot dog's ingredients—everything that may legally qualify—because it was asked by the poultry industry to relax the conditions under which these ingredients might also include chicken. In other words, can a chickenfurter find happiness in the land of the frank?

Judging by the 1,066 mainly hostile answers that the Department got when it sent out a questionnaire on this point, the very thought is unthinkable. The public mood was most felicitously caught by the woman who replied: "I don't eat feather meat of no kind."

A proud credo. Obviously she regards feather meat as beneath contempt—maybe she doesn't know that the feathers are removed first—and feels that only the hot dog is worthy of her fastidious taste. Yet the official list of what may constitute a hot dog is not my idea of nature's aristocracy:

> The edible part of the muscle of cattle, sheep, swine, or goats, in the diaphragm, in the heart, or in the esophagus, with or without the accompanying and overlying fat, and the portions of bone, skin, sinew, nerve and blood vessels which normally accompany the muscle tissue and which are not separated from it by the process of dressing. It does not include the muscle found in the lips, snout or ears.

Well, thank God for that last sentence anyway. I'll go along with the goatfurter—in fact, I'm sure I often have. But I draw the line at lipfurters and snoutfurters, and as for earfurters, I can only say, "I don't eat ear meat of no kind."

What the Department of Agriculture finally decided was to let frankfurters be called frankfurters even if they contain up to 15 percent chicken. The old rule said that the label had to announce, in large type: FRANKFURTER, CHICKEN ADDED.

It may seem like a small point—mere semantic quibbling—but clearly it is not. Whole philosophical questions are at stake, and so is the American way of life. For although the frankfurter originated in Frankfurt, we have long since made it our own, a twin pillar of democracy along with Mom's apple pie. In fact, now that Mom's apple pie comes frozen and baked by somebody who isn't Mom, the hot dog stands alone. What it symbolizes remains pure, even if what it contains does not.

This is why the poultry interests were so eager to get rid of the terrible words CHICKEN ADDED, when chicken is added. They know that Americans will eat absolutely anything which is labeled FRANKFURTER, but will often balk if they learn that it once had feathers. Maybe what the poultry people really need is not a change of label but a change of press agents to improve the chicken's image. Any branch of the food industry that allows itself to be upstaged by the diaphragm of a goat or the esophagus of a swine has plenty of work to do.

Meanwhile the hot dog rides above the strife, unassailable, the only item in cookery which compensates as an institution for what it frequently lacks as food. Didn't President Roosevelt give hot dogs to George V when England's king and queen came here in 1939 to cement the alliance? But if Roosevelt had gone to England, would the king have given him beef and kidney pie? Not if he wanted those fifty destroyers.

Even today American chief executives regard the frankfurter as their proper domain, as President Nixon proved when he set the fat level at 30 percent last year, ending a dispute that raged simultaneously with the chicken controversy but didn't match it for disgusting details. Nixon's special assistant for consumer affairs, Mrs. Virginia Knauer, says that he telephoned her one night and announced, "I'm with you 100 percent on the hot dog issue"—possibly the most decisive statement he has made on anything so far.

Partly, of course, the hot dog is triumphant because it is so easy to manage. Unlike the chicken, which has just enough grease to drip on a clean dress and just too many bones to put into one's pocket, the frank comes wrapped in its own napkin and is soon gone without a trace. It is the ultimate food of the disposable society.

It is also, like the Bill of Rights, always there when you need it. No public or sporting event is so meager, no recreational facility so minimal, that a vendor is not nearby with the edible part of the muscle of cattle, sheep, swine or goats. Broadway and Coney Island are practically paved with hot dogs. Who would be so un-American, therefore, as to question what goes into them? If the taste seems a little heavy on the esophagus side, or tilted more toward goat than cattle, that's what mustard is for.

Is It an O.K. Word, Usewise?

WILL I ACCEPT the verb "to host"? Or "escalate" or "finalize" or "enthuse"? Do I approve of nouns posing as adjectives: "health reasons" or "disaster proportions"? How do I feel about "it's me"? Will I allow "like" to be used as a conjunction—like so many people do? Will I give my O.K. to "mighty," as in "mighty fine"? Will I give my O.K. to "O.K."?

I received these questions in the mail for four years, and so did 103 other men and women, a group of people —mostly writers, poets, editors and teachers—who care about the language and try to use it well. We are the "panel on usage" formed by a new dictionary—*The American Heritage Dictionary of the English Language*—to appraise the new words and dubious constructions that have come knocking at the door. Which should be ushered in, which thrown out on their ear?

Now that the Dictionary has been born we can see what we decided. Even before publication it was clear that our passions ran high, for some of the comments that we wrote on our questionnaires were released to the press. "Good God, no! Never!" cried Barbara W. Tuchman, asked about the verb "to author." Scholarship hath no fury like that of a language purist confronted with sludge, and I share Miss Tuchman's vow that "author" shall never be authorized, just as I agree with Lewis Mumford that the adverb "good" should be "left as the exclusive property of Hemingway" and with Gerald Carson that "normalcy" should be "permitted only to admirers of the late Warren G. Harding."

But a usage panel is only doing half its job if it merely keeps the language from becoming sloppy. Any boob can rule that the suffix "wise," as in "mediawise," is boobwise, or that being "rather unique" is no more possible than being rather pregnant. The other half of the job is to help the language grow by welcoming any newcomer that will bring strength or color.

Therefore I was glad to see in the Dictionary that 97 percent of us voted to admit "dropout," which is clean and vivid, but only 47 percent would accept "senior citizen," which is pretentious and patronizing, typical of all the pudgy new intruders from the land of sociology, where a clod is an underachiever and a slum is a depressed socioeconomic area. I'm glad we accepted "escalate," the kind of verbal contraption which I ordinarily dislike, but which the Vietnam war has given a precise meaning, complete with overtones of blunder.

I'm glad we took into full membership all sorts of robust words that were formerly degraded as "colloquial":

adjectives like "rambunctious," verbs like "stall" and "trigger" and "rile," nouns like "shambles" and "tycoon" and "trek," the latter approved by 78 percent to mean any difficult trip, as in "the commuter's daily trek to Manhattan." Originally, of course, it was a Cape Dutch word applied to the Boers' harsh journey by ox wagon. But who is to say that the Manhattan commuter's daily trek is any less arduous, or made on trains that are much better than an ox wagon? Not us.

This is the virtue of having a usage panel and tabulating its opinions in the dictionary: it puts our differences on display as well as our agreements. Thus our 95 percent vote against "myself," as in "he invited Mary and myself to dinner," condemned as "prissy," "horrible" and "a genteelism," ought to warn off anyone who doesn't want to be prissy, horrible and genteel. As Red Smith put it, " 'Myself' is the refuge of idiots taught early that 'me' is a dirty word."

On the other hand, only 66 percent of us rejected the verb "to contact," and only half opposed the split infinitive and the verbs "to fault" and "to bus." So nobody can really fault you if you decide to willingly contact your school board and bus your children to another town. Our apparent rule of thumb was stated by Theodore M. Bernstein: "We should apply the test of convenience and necessity. Does the word fill a real need? If it does, let's give it a franchise."

All of this merely confirms what any lexicographer knows: that the laws of usage are relative, bending with the taste of the lawmaker. Katherine Anne Porter calls "O.K." a "detestable vulgarity" and claims that she has never spoken the word in her life, whereas I will freely admit that I have spoken the word "O.K." "Most," as in "most everyone," was derided as "cute farmer talk" by

Isaac Asimov and embraced as a "good English idiom" by Virgil Thomson. "Regime," meaning any administration, as in "the Kennedy regime," drew the approval of most everyone on the panel—as did "dynasty"—and the wrath of Jacques Barzun, who said, "These are technical terms, you blasted non-historians!" I railed against the bloated noun "personality," as in a "TV personality," but now I wonder if it isn't the only word for that vast new breed of people who are famous for being famous—and, quite possibly, for nothing else. What does Art Linkletter, for instance, really *do*? Or Zsa Zsa Gabor?

In the end it comes down to one question: what is "correct" usage? We have no king to establish the King's English; we only have the President's English—which we don't want. Webster, long a defender of the faith, roiled the waters in 1961 with its permissive Third Edition, which argued that almost anything goes as long as somebody uses it, noting that "ain't" is "used orally in most parts of the U.S. by many cultivated speakers."

Just where Webster cultivated those speakers I ain't sure. Nevertheless it's true that the spoken language is always looser than the written language, and *The American Heritage Dictionary* properly put its questions to us in both forms. Often we gladly allowed an oral idiom which we forbade in print as too informal, fully realizing, however, that "the pen must at length comply with the tongue," as Samuel Johnson said, and that today's garbage may be gold tomorrow. Usewise, some of it just can't be finalized.

We also recognized that usage can vary within a given word. We voted heavily against "cohort" as a synonym for "colleague"—except where the tone was jocular. Thus a professor would not be among his cohorts at a faculty meeting, but they would abound at his college reunion, probably wearing funny hats. We rejected "too" as a common synonym for "very," as in "his health is not too good." Whose health is? But we approved it in wry or humorous use: "He was not too happy when she ignored him."

On the whole our panel turned out to be liberal in accepting new words and phrases, but conservative in grammar. We strictly upheld most of the classic distinctions ("can" and "may," "fewer" and "less," etc.) and decried the classic errors, insisting that "flaunt" still doesn't mean "flout," or "infer" mean "imply," that "fortuitous" still means "accidental" and "disinterested" means "impartial," no matter how many people use them wrong. Or wrongly. Here we were motivated by our love of the language's beautiful precision. Like any craftsmen, we enjoy using exact tools and hate to see them maltreated. "Simple illiteracy," Dwight Macdonald said, "is no basis for linguistic evolution."

"I choose always the grammatical form unless it sounds affected," explained Marianne Moore, and that, finally, is where we took our stand. We are not pedants, so hung up on correctness that we don't want the language to keep refreshing itself with phrases like "hung up." That doesn't mean, however, that we have to accept every atrocity that comes along, like "hopefully." Prayerfully these usages can be kept out, but fearfully many of them won't be.

The Truth About Walt Disney

WALT DISNEY sure had me fooled. I always thought he was an Establishment square, the pious merchant of every virtue that middle America cherishes and young America hates. Who else could make cuteness so commercial? Or extract so many millions from a mouse?

But suddenly the young have embraced this king of squares. His *Fantasia* was revived recently at a New York theater and, overnight, there they were, lined up outside, the beaded and bearded Aquarians, making such a box-office hit of the thirty-year-old film that it is now being booked into cities and college towns all across the country.

Obviously *Fantasia* is saying something to the young in 1970 that it wasn't saying to me—or anyone—in 1940. I remember it then for its heavy cultural pretensions:

Uncle Walt bringing good music to the masses by wrapping it in easy-to-take animated cartoons. The other day I went to the movie again and saw just what the young have instead discovered—that Disney was zonked out of his mind while making the movie and so was his entire studio. Safely hidden behind the chaste pillars of classical music, behind the impeccable tails of Leopold Stokowski, he was a hippie thirty years ahead of his time, producing a psychedelic light-and-sound show that was his only flop because nobody was freaked out enough to dig it. It's like finding out that J. Edgar Hoover reads Marcuse under the covers at night.

Knowing this, I now feel sorry for Disney. It's no fun to be a secret pioneer. In *Fantasia* he anticipated by a whole generation the ideas that were to bestow instant priesthood on Marshall McLuhan and Timothy Leary, on Allen Ginsberg and Alan Watts, and he died without getting any of the credit. Long before TV made us a visual society feeding on picture images, long before McLuhan announced that "the medium is the message" and the printed word is out, Disney was giving us a sensory experience, America's first acid happening.

Don't get hung up looking for a story, he was saying—this is no linear arrangement of one thought after another. Just drench your senses in these bright shifting colors and in these enveloping waves of sound, and that's all the story you need. Tune in and turn on. A quarter of a century later Bill Graham opened the Fillmore Auditorium in San Francisco to provide the same kind of mind-blowing trip and everybody said he was a genius. But Disney was the genius. If ever a piece of real estate deserved his name, it's the Fillmore. Instead he's stuck with Disneyland.

Analyze *Fantasia* and it's unmistakable that Disney was

one of the Now People way back then. There's not a straight line in the whole film. Everything wiggles or ripples or flows, starting with the very first frame of Bach's Toccata and Fugue in D Minor, which I thought was a very orderly piece of work. So what's on the screen? Liquid patterns to represent the flowing notes. Rolling billows and curves and undulating lines. Sharp bursts of brilliant color, all building to a climax of swirling clouds and a flaming sun. That's a toccata?

Next comes Tchaikovsky's *The Nutcracker Suite*—but not the boring old *Nutcracker* that we take our children to see. This is pure flower-child stuff. First, the Dance of the Sugar Plum Fairy, who sparkles all over (early "ecstatic dress"). Then the Chinese Dance (hip mushrooms), the Dance of the Reed Flutes (psychedelic blossoms), the Arabian Dance (squirming goldfish), the Russian Dance (thistles swing with orchids), and finally the Waltz of the Flowers, in which the autumn fairies open milkweed pods to set free the seeds. So Walt was into sunflowers and peyote, too. From there it's a fast dissolve into Dukas's *The Sorcerer's Apprentice* (Mickey Mouse amid rushing waters) and Stravinsky's *Rite of Spring*, nothing less than the struggle of the earth itself to be born. No hard edges here—it's red molten lava, whirling gases, boiling seas and wriggling protoplasm.

But all this is mere warm-up for Beethoven's *Pastoral Symphony*, where Disney not only keeps up the visual assault but socks us with the very life-styles of today's Woodstock generation. Nudity, communes, love-ins, return to nature, revolt against authority—it's all there. Of course Disney had to present it in a setting that wouldn't offend the morality of an era that wasn't ready for him, and he cleverly chose Greek mythology. We all study those myths in grammar school—what could be safer?

Plenty. You've never seen so many bare-breasted girl centaurs and bare-behinded cherubs, such grooving and group therapy on the unpolluted slopes of Olympus, such tripping on grapes, and the whole thing ends with Bacchus and his girl defying Zeus, the military-industrial Establishment figure who tries to restore law and order by having thunderbolts thrown at the hippies down below. It's confrontation politics, and the thunderbolts keep missing—which shows where Disney's sentiments lay. Make love, not war, Zeus. Turn on, baby.

I won't describe any more. Enough to say that there was no relief, either in Moussorgsky's *Night on Bald Mountain* (jiggling spirits) or Schubert's *Ave Maria* (flickering candles), and when I staggered up the theater aisle, past the smoking section where the smoke didn't smell like tobacco, I was grateful to get out into the streets of Manhattan, where soot had turned the bright blue sky to gray and congestion kept the traffic from moving. There's a price for withdrawal from the wonderful world of Walt Disney.

Still, I can't say that he didn't try again and again to tip us off. He made one whole movie about a commune—*Snow White and the Seven Dwarfs*—but none of the characters was ever shown in the nude, so nobody dug what a beautiful scene it really was. And in *Alice in Wonderland* he made a mushroom sequence so spaced-out that the Jefferson Airplane ran it in a concert last fall to get the audience turned on for their rock hit "White Rabbit." That's when the Aquarians finally woke up to the truth about Uncle Walt.

Disney, however, was no longer around. He died straight, without knowing that his private visions would soon become public experience, identified at the end with

Mary Poppins, one of the straightest characters he ever brought to the screen.

But was she? Mary Poppins sang an entire song to explain that "a spoonful of sugar makes the medicine go down." By then every magazine had visited the Haight-Ashbury district and described how LSD was being routinely taken in sugar cubes, and still we all thought she really meant sugar. It must have driven Walt crazy.

Perelman Revisited

I BECAME a teen-age addict in the late 1930s when I began to notice in *The New Yorker* certain sentences that were unlike any that I had ever seen before, or even imagined. They kept turning up in pieces by a man who signed himself S. J. Perelman, and they just plain fractured me. I memorized whole patches of them and even started to talk in imitation Perelmanese, a habit that was considered attractive by nobody.

Now suddenly it is thirty years later and S. (for Sidney) J. (for Joseph) Perelman (for Perelman) is sixty-six. He is still doing business at the old stand; and I am still a teen-age addict—it is only by pure will power that I can resist describing the old stand that he is still doing business at. I'm stuck with my adolescent crush on a writer who put the language through some of its most breathtaking loops and, in the process, changed the shape of twentieth-century humor. Today in both America and England the woods are full of writers and comics who were drawn into the gravitational pull of Perelman's style and never quite got back out.

Typical of the sentences that hooked me were the following, and anyone who doesn't think they are funny might as well get out of the car right here and walk to the nearest book on muncipal bonds or the SEATO alliance. No amount of time or money will buy their goodwill.

> Women loved this impetual Irish adventurer who would rather fight than eat and vice-versa. One night he was chafing at The Bit, a tavern in Portsmouth, when he overheard a chance remark from a brawny gunner's mate in his cups. . . .
>
> The following morning the "Maid of Hull," a frigate of the line mounting 36 guns, out of Bath and into bed in a twinkling, dropped downstream on the tide, bound for Bombay, object matrimony. On her as passenger went my grandfather. Fifty-three days later he was heading for the interior of one of the Northern states. Living almost entirely on cameo brooches and the few ptarmigan which fell to the ptrigger of his pfowling piece, he at last sighted the towers of Ishpeming, the Holy City of the Surds and Cosines, fanatic Mohammedan warrior sects.

> "Jelly sandwiches! Oh, Moms!"
>
> "Eat them all, boy o' mine," she told me, "they're good for boys with hollow little legs." Tenderly she pinned to my lapel the green tag reading "To Plushnick Productions, Hollywood, California." The whistle shrilled and in a moment I was chugging out of Grand Central's dreaming spires. I had chugged only a few feet when I realized I had left without the train, so I had to run back and wait for it to start. . . .
>
> I noted with pleasure that a fresh coat of grime had been given to the Dearborn Street station, though I was hardly

vain enough to believe that it had anything to do with my visit. . . . "General Crook," in whom I was to make my home for the next three days, and his two neighbors, "Lake Tahoe" and "Chief Malomai," were everything that the word "Pullman" implies; they were Pullmans.

The scene could have been staged only by a Lubitsch; in fact, Lubitsch himself was seated on a bench across the street, smoking a cucumber and looking as cool as a cigar. It lacked only Nelson Eddy to appear on a penthouse terrace and loose a chorus of deep-throated song, and, as if by magic, Nelson Eddy suddenly appeared on a penthouse terrace and, with the artistry that has made his name a word, launched into an aria.

"I'm sorry," he added Quigley.

"Why did you add Quigley?" I begged him. He apologized and subtracted Quigley, then divided Hogan. . . .

"Are you mad, Russell?" I stopped him haughtily. He bit his lip in a manner which awakened my maternal sympathy, and I helped him bite it.

What hooked me about these sentences was that they revealed whole new possibilities of written humor, and therefore of pleasure for the reader. I saw that anything was possible if a writer threw off the chains of logic and let his mind work by free association, ricocheting from the normal to the absurd and usually destroying, by the very unexpectedness of its angle, whatever trite or pompous idea had been there before.

I began to see that the essence of humor was surprise. Perelman would catch the reader off balance with a jagged turn and never look back. If the reader also made the turn he was a happy man, and that's what the game was all about. If he didn't, there was no point in going back to pick him up; he would only miss it again.

Thus it dawned on me—and this is what has held my admiration for Perelman ever since—that a great humorist operates on a deeper current than most people suspect: pure courage. No other kind of writer risks his neck so visibly or so often on the high wire of public approval. It is the thinnest wire in all literature, and the writer lives with the certain knowledge that he will frequently fall off. Yet he is deadly serious, this acrobat teetering over our heads, or he wouldn't keep going back out, trying to startle us with nonsense into seeing our lives with sense.

For this perpetual act of courage and commitment the humorist's reward in America is to be dismissed as a trifler, someone who never settled down to "important" work. One can scan forever the list of writers who won the Pulitzer Prize or some other literary honor without finding George Ade, Ring Lardner, Robert Benchley, James Thurber, S. J. Perelman or any other humorist.

Yet who is to say that they are not among our most valuable resources? Not me. And not, ironically, the English. Perelman is a literary hero in Great Britain. T. S. Eliot and Somerset Maugham were among his many friends and admirers there, and Spike Milligan and Peter Sellers, architects of the BBC's "Goon Show," which kept England doubled up in the 1950s, acknowledge Perelman as their mentor.

In America, however, the humorist sits holding his hat at the reception desk, a queer bird, not quite to be trusted, or, above all, paid homage. Well, let other pilgrims go to Oxford, Miss., or Asheville, N.C. My own literary shrine is outside Erwinna, Pa.—and it is not hard to be outside Erwinna, Pa.—where Perelman lives in an old farmhouse with two enormous poodles. His wife, Laura, who was his collaborator on many plays and screenplays, died earlier this year. Their two grown children now live elsewhere, and the mynah bird that they got in Siam in 1949 has died. A spectacular attempt to redress its loss took place last year when Perelman, an avid subscriber to *La Vie des Bêtes,* noticed that his barn was exactly as long as a gibbon's swing, 34 feet, and set out to buy a pair of siamang gibbons. "I also wanted to find if there was a decent young black panther available in Bangkok," he says, "and then pick up a cheetah in East Africa on the way home." But the plan miscarried, and Perelman remains birdless and apeless in Erwinna.

There, the other day, he looked back over a life that has included writing movies for the Marx Brothers and sailing to Zanzibar on an Arab dhow, two adventures that he recalls with equal loathing, though, given a choice, he would rather talk about the dhow. He has visited most of the exotic corners of the world that first caught his fancy in the tinted prose of Sax Rohmer and H. Rider Haggard, and perhaps no other writer—as his writings testify—has so broad and recondite a knowledge of travel. I once took a copra boat through the Moluccas solely because he told me it was a great trip (it was), and he has also steered me to interesting people in cities from Nairobi to Jakarta, sending letters ahead to ease my journey. He is a generous man in his affection for friends and his enthusiasm for far places. "It would give me more satisfaction," he says, "to walk down Ice House Street in Hong Kong in a white drill suit than to own the Chevrolet dealership in Sheboygan, Wisconsin."

Reluctantly I dragged his thoughts back to Providence, where he grew up, as his fans well know from such opening sentences as this: "I'm no bloody hero, and when the Princess Pats stood at Passchendaele in '17, I was damned careful to be twelve years old and three thousand miles to the rear, selling Domes of Silence after school to the housewives of Crescent Park, Rhode Island."

"My father had a speckled career," he said. "He owned a dry goods store and was a machinist and an unsuccessful poultryman. It was the American dream that if you had a few acres and a chicken farm there was no limit to your possible wealth. I grew up with and have since retained the keenest hatred of chickens. My chief interest always was to be a cartoonist, and I began very early to draw cartoons in my father's store on the long cardboard strips around which the bolts of Amoskeag cotton and ginghams were stored.

"I also became a great reader as soon as I was able to appreciate the beauty of Horatio Alger and Oliver Optic and books like *Toby Tyler, or Ten Weeks with a Circus*. And there was an absolute smasher of a romantic novel called *In the Sargasso Sea*, by Janvier. I checked recently at the Providence Public Library and found that it has only been taken out twice since. I was able to recognize the very smear of chicken fat that my greasy fingers had imprisoned on the flyleaf."

At about eleven he graduated to the material that he regards as "without question, my formative education"—the chestnuts which, long afterward, in the series called *Cloudland Revisited*, he gulped down once again and found to be chestnuts. They were books like *Graustark, Girl of the Limberlost, Trail of the Lonesome Pine, The Woman Thou Gavest, The Mystery of Dr. Fu Manchu, Three Weeks, The Winning of Barbara Worth, Scaramouche, Pollyanna* and dozens of others beyond remembering, except by Perelman, who suffers from total recall.

"It was nothing at all for people who liked reading," he says, "to go to the public library on Friday with a book strap and bring home seven or eight books. Then you'd sit all weekend with your feet in the oven and your eyes protruding a half-inch from their sockets, wolfing ginger snaps, and finish them all. So instead of engaging in healthy blood sports, as I might have if I'd been an English boy, I was filling up my mind with all this mulch."

A second layer of mulch, equally important to future growth, soon followed the first—silent films, an era symbolized in Perelman's studio today by a photograph of Jetta Goudal. "She was the great crypto-Eurasian vampire of all time," he says. "Actually she was a Jewish girl named Yetta who took her last name from the Dutch cheese. She really ignited me in *Java Head,* playing this tootsie who's brought back from the East Indies. I was also successively in love with Corinne Griffith ('the orchidaceous star'), Priscilla Dean, Aileen Pringle and Nita Naldi, down whom, as I once wrote, it was my boyhood ambition to coast on a Flexible Flyer."

In 1921 Perelman went to Brown, where he found his direction by working on its humor magazine, *The Brown Jug,* as a cartoonist and later as editor. He recalls John Held, Jr., as the biggest influence on college humor. "He had a deep knowledge of the flapper and the collegian and the sharpie, and he represented them in a sociological way that had tremendous humor—the flappers, for instance, in their Bramley dresses with yoke collars and accordion-pleated skirts and their open galoshes and their hair done in 'cootie garages' and spit curls. Held brought into focus everything that was going on with young people."

Not until mid-college did the eventual writer meet his first literary influence or try any writing. "H. L. Mencken was the Catherine wheel, the ultimate firework," Perelman says. "He loosened up journalism. With his use of the colloquial and the dynamic, the foreign reference, and the bizarre word like *Sitzfleisch,* he brought adrenalin into the gray and pulpy style of the day. Under his influence I wrote editorials advocating, of course, the dismissal of the dean and all the other pompous old foofs on the faculty."

Still, Perelman remained a cartoonist at heart and was thrilled, upon graduating, to get a letter from Norman Anthony, editor of *Judge*. "I tied a red bandanna to a peeled willow stick and emigrated to New York in 1925 to earn, as I believed, a sumptuous living at that magazine. I saw myself ensconced in a studio with lightly draped models, wearing a Windsor tie and a beret and expertly negotiating a palette, a loaded brush and a maulstick.

"What I didn't know was that I was hitching my star to a wagon that was gathering night soil. *Judge* was the most insolvent of magazines. Its treasurer, Joseph Cooney, had a gray suit, and they painted the office gray to make him invisible. Hirelings waiting to be paid would see a red spot moving along the wall, but by the time they realized it was Cooney's ruddy face he was out the door. I was there from 1925 to 1929 and had a contract to provide two cartoons and one humor piece every week."

Seen today, the cartoons—relying on wheezy two-liners and terrible puns—seem so callow that one wonders about the state of magazine humor in the sainted twenties. Typical is a drawing of a pasha saying to his vizier, "Who's been eating my Kurds and why?" As for the humor pieces, they aren't much better, and it is not until 1930, when he went to *College Humor*, that the genuine original S. J. Perelman begins to materialize in print.

"I was beginning to develop a sense of parody and of lapidary prose," he says.

Enter the Marx Brothers. "They were feverish to get

into radio," Perelman recalls, "and they detailed me and Will B. Johnstone, another comic artist, to contrive a program. We had a conception of them as four stowaways immersed in the hold of a transatlantic liner, and there our invention stopped. They said, 'This isn't our radio show, it's our next movie.' They took us up to Jesse Lasky in the Paramount building, and three weeks later we were barreling westward on the Chief to write *Monkey Business.*

"Meanwhile the Marxes took off to play the Palladium in London, where they were a dazzling failure. I can't tell you how badly they were received—audiences threw pennies at them—which is ironic because they're idols there today. Well, when they got back they summoned us for a reading of our script. They came with their lawyers and accountants and masseurs and dentists—twenty-three people, plus Zeppo's two afghans and Chico's schnauzer—and I read for eighty-five minutes in absolute silence. At the end Chico said, 'Whaddya think, Grouch?' Groucho took the cigar out of his mouth and said, 'Stinks!', and they all got up and walked out. So we started again, and in 1931 the picture was done and was a hit."

The next year the Marxes signed him—and Bert Kalmar and Harry Ruby—to write *Horse Feathers,* a comedy distinguished, as all good Marxists know, by such exchanges as this:

SECRETARY: Jennings is waxing wroth outside.
GROUCHO: Well, tell Roth to wax Jennings for a while.

"But nothing would impel me ever to work for them again," Perelman says.

So began a decade of going out to Hollywood, which he once described as "a dreary industrial town controlled by hoodlums of enormous wealth," to work on perishable films with titles like *Florida Special* and *Ambush* ("Laura and I were supposed to introduce the humorous element"). At one point they were hired by Irving Thalberg at M-G-M "to work on a loathsome little thing called *Greenwich Village* because we had once lived on Washington Square." They also wrote such screenplays as *Sweethearts,* hardly the most urbane of films, and Perelman once found himself put to work on *How to Win Friends and Influence People,* intended as a vehicle for Joan Crawford and Fanny Brice and, he says, "mercifully never completed. Scholars today refer to the thirties as the golden age of Hollywood. Purest nonsense. It was assembly-line stuff, just people doing a job."

Such satisfactions as he has won in dramatic form have come from several Broadway comedies written with his wife; from the hit musical *One Touch of Venus,* written with Ogden Nash; from his own play, *The Beauty Part,* and from the Academy Award-winning script of Michael Todd's *Around the World in 80 Days.* And he has his memories: of conferring with Todd around a pool in Palm Springs, for instance, and of Elizabeth Taylor "lying on a couch like Madame Récamier, spooning in this particolored ice cream that an insolent Mexican chauffeur had brought nine miles and reading a copy of *The Bride Wore Black,* by Cornell Woolrich, upside down. Actually she only knows three words: Van Cleef and Arpels."

All of this, however, has been diversionary—and who is more diversionary than Elizabeth Taylor on a couch? —to the main thread of Perelman's work, the steady spinning out of humor pieces, or, as he puts it, "laboriously sewing on bugle beads." The targets of his humor have changed since he started writing for *The New Yorker* in 1934, but not the identifying marks of his style—the boundless word play ("my whipcords stood out like veins"), the rich invention of proper names like Lucas Membrane and the Yale Lox Associates, and the immense fund of words that are not only esoteric but precise.

"Sid commands a vocabulary," says E. B. White, "that is the despair (and joy) of every writing man. He is like a Roxy organ that has three decks, fifty stops and a pride of pedals under the bench. When he wants a word it's there. He and Laura showed up at our house in Sarasota a couple of winters ago. They had been in an automobile accident—a bad one, the car a complete wreck. Laura came out of it with some bruises, Sid with a new word. The car, he learned, had been 'totaled.' I could see that the addition of this word to his already enormous store meant a lot to him. His ears are as busy as an ant's feelers. No word ever gets by him."

In the beginning Perelman was preoccupied, he says, with the absurdities of advertising—"advertisers in the thirties were giving themselves the most colossal airs, bombinating away about the creative importance of what they were doing." He also dipped heavily into the pretentious world of trade magazines like *Oral Hygiene* and women's magazines like *Harper's Bazaar*—mere warm-ups, as it turned out, for a later satire that impaled the lady editor of *Flair* magazine (or was it *Fleur* magazine?), called "The Hand That Cradles the Rock."

"Then I got off on the nostalgia kick, revisiting the books and films of my boyhood. There was a kind of marsh gas that had begun to glow over those early movies, seen across the perspective of twenty-five or thirty years: a delicious humor in their crudities and their bravura. At that time, of course, there wasn't all this punditry on old films." Perelman's tolerance for today's turgid scholars of the cinema is not high. Still, it's possible that he started the whole vogue. If so, it is because he looked at his material with the special vision of the humorist and thereby saw it true—which is the greatness, he feels, of the humorists he himself most admires.

"George Ade was my first influence as a humorist," he says. "He had a social sense of history. His pictures of Hoosier life at the turn of the century, as in the fable of 'The Waist-Band That Was Taut,' are more documentary than any of those studies on how much people paid for their coal. Ade's humor was rooted in a perception of people and places. He had a cutting edge and an acerbic wit that no earlier American humorist had.

"Generally speaking, I don't believe in kindly humor. I don't think it exists. One of the most shameful utterances to stem from the human mouth is Will Rogers' 'I never met a man I didn't like.' The absolute antithesis is Oscar Wilde on the foxhunting Englishman: 'the unspeakable in full pursuit of the uneatable.' The two examples sum up, for me, the distinction. Wilde's remark contains, in the briefest span, the truth; whereas Rogers' is pure flatulence, crowd-pleasing and fake humility."

Other early influences on Perelman were Stephen Leacock, Max Beerbohm, Lardner, Benchley, Donald Ogden Stewart and Frank Sullivan. A later hero was, and still is, Raymond Chandler. "He took the private-eye legend, which had been invented by Dashiell Hammett, and refined it and added an element that was not very obvious, and that was humor." (Perelman's affection for Chandler shines through his brilliant parody, "Farewell, My Lovely Appetizer.") E. M. Forster is another hero—"his story, 'Luncheon at Pretoria,' is one of the finest pieces of comic writing I know"—and so is Henry David Thoreau. "But the greatest was James Joyce. I've come over the years to realize that *Ulysses* is the greatest work of the comic imagination that exists for me.

"Humor is purely a point of view, and only the pedants try to classify it. For me its chief merit is the use of the unexpected, the glancing allusion, the deflation of pomposity, and the constant repetition of one's helplessness in a majority of situations. One doesn't consciously start out wanting to be a social satirist. You find something absurd enough to make you want to push a couple of antipersonnel bombs under it. If it then seems to have another element of meaning, that's lagniappe. But the main obligation is to amuse yourself."

E. B. White, reflecting on Perelman's career, says, "I'm sure Sid's stuff influenced me in the early days. His pieces usually had a lead sentence, or lead paragraph, that was as hair-raising as the first big dip on a roller coaster: it got you in the stomach, and when it was over you were relieved to feel deceleration setting in. In the realm of satire, parody and burlesque, he has, from the beginning, bowed to none. His erudition is as impressive as his flights of fancy. I don't like the word 'humorist,' never have. It seems to me misleading. Humor is a by-product that occurs in the serious work of some and not others. I was more influenced by Don Marquis than by Ernest Hemingway, by Perelman than by Dreiser."

White, of course, went on to practice many forms of writing, which he did superbly, and Benchley once claimed that he was influenced out of business altogether. "It was just a matter of time," he said, "before Perelman took over the *dementia praecox* field and drove us all to writing articles on economics."

So it might seem that Perelman today is the last of the

breed. Actually he is and always has been the only member of his breed, sui generis to a fault. He doesn't even look like anyone else: the copious eyebrows and moustache, the ample forehead, the thin and lively face, the small metal-rimmed glasses which he bought in Paris in 1927 and which now draw the admiring stares of hippies whose own glasses aren't as cool. His clothes are chosen, in London, with the same elegant taste that goes into his choosing of words—they are quirky but exactly right, making him that rarest of literary hands, a dapper one.

Even the trade that he plies, Perelman feels, is at the edge of extinction. "Humor that's destined for print has almost entirely disappeared because of the growth of communication. What passes for humor on TV doesn't deserve the name." Nevertheless he has started on a major work destined for print, his autobiography, to be called *The Hindsight Saga.*

Sometimes I hear people say that Perelman is no longer as funny. How could he be? The early Perelman was the funniest man alive, and inevitably some of the surprise is gone because he has taught us over two generations to expect the unexpected, to stay loose. Inevitably, too, his writing has deepened with travel and scholarship. Its texture is richer, its surface less gaudy.

But the biggest difference is not that humor has gone out of the humorist, but that the world has taken over his work. Life today has become so preposterous that it outstrips comic invention. It is its own comment. The real miracle is that Perelman keeps going out on the wire. I watch him with continuing wonder and gratitude, and I wouldn't trade my addiction for anybody else's.

Mowbot, Get Lost

SUMMER IS GONE and I still haven't seen my first Mowbot. The Mowbot is a new cordless electric mower that will cut your grass automatically—it's a small and shapeless creature that looks newly arrived from Mars—and maybe the reason I haven't seen it is that it costs $975. But I really don't think this is a question of money. It's a religious issue.

Consider what the manufacturers suggest in their ads: "Start it and go off to your foursome, come back and your lawn's manicured." That sounds appealing enough—the ultimate dream of a society in headlong pursuit of leisure. But will the owner be happy out on the golf course, knowing that he has run away from the one act by which America judges the moral fitness of her citizens? Not a chance. Let a man drink or default, cheat on his taxes or cheat on his wife, and the community will find forgiveness in its heart. But let him fail to keep his front lawn mowed, and to be seen doing it, and those hearts will turn to stone.

For the American front lawn is a holy place, constantly worshiped but never used. Only its high priest, the husband, may set foot on it, and then only to perform the sacred rites—mowing with a mower, edging with an edger, sprinkling with a hose, and rooting with a rooter to purify the temple of profane weeds. The rest of the family reaches the house via a cement walk, and if Dad and Mom want to enjoy their lawn they sit in the garage, side by side in camp chairs, and look at it.

Sometimes, driving through a suburb, I see an object that has been left on the front lawn by mistake, and I think how everyone on the block must hate that house. It wouldn't take more than five or six such objects to turn the neighbors as ugly as a lynch mob. And if they were to see a man's lawn being mowed by an automatic mower after he had driven off with his golf clubs, no force on earth could stop them from descending on it with sledgehammers and smashing its electronic brain.

That's why I haven't seen my first Mowbot. If it's cutting any grass in America, it's cutting the grass out behind—a secular area where people may sit or sprawl, eat or drink, and even cook. The trouble is that this space is doubly cluttered, being the repository for all the normal props of outdoor living that could be spread equally between the front lawn and the back. Just to clear this rear yard for the Mowbot to cut would be more work for the man of the house than to cut the grass himself.

He knows from experience, after all, how to steer his lawn mower around the dismembered dolls and miniature dump trucks, the plastic dog bones and the barbecue grill, the collapsible canvas chair that doesn't collapse and the inflatable rubber pool that does. Would the Mowbot know as much? Its manufacturers claim that it avoids all obstacles, including pets and toys, and that it won't touch shrubs or flowers. Simply (they say) place the electronic signal wire around the area that you want cut, turn the Mowbot on, and go take a nap.

But how well will I sleep, knowing that I've left my property in charge of a machine—one that doesn't make any sound? Are its sensors *really* avoiding my pets and toys? And my children? And how about the car? Move it to a neighbor's driveway? Or has the Mowbot already eaten its tires? What else did I leave out there on the grass? My sneakers! Good-bye, old friends—you've been turned into mulch by now. And Grandma? Which side of the electronic signal wire is *she* on? Last time I saw her she was darning socks. Maybe that was the last time I saw her.

And is the Mowbot making value judgments on the litter of my interior life—shredding my baseball magazines but leaving *Ada* untouched, though I'd rather find *Ada* gone without a trace? What if I come out and find the Mowbot itself gone without a trace? For the owner's manual mentions what to do if it "crosses signal wire."

That's no way to get any sleep. I'd lie awake the entire time, wondering where my lawn mower was, torturing myself with worry, waiting for the dreaded phone call: "This is Chief Callahan down at the station house. We just caught your Mowbot breaking and entering over on Elm Street. It mowed a mink coat, two poodles and a wall-to-wall carpet."

The Right to Fail

I LIKE "DROPOUT" as an addition to the American language because it's brief and it's clear. What I don't like is that we use it almost entirely as a dirty word.

We only apply it to people under twenty-one. Yet an adult who spends his days and nights watching mindless TV programs is more of a dropout than an eighteen-year-old who quits college, with its frequently mindless courses, to become, say, a VISTA volunteer. For the young, dropping out is often a way of dropping in.

To hold this opinion, however, is little short of treason in America. A boy or girl who leaves college is branded a failure—and the right to fail is one of the few freedoms that this country does not grant its citizens. The American dream is a dream of "getting ahead," painted in strokes of gold wherever we look. Our advertisements and TV commercials are a hymn to material success, our magazine articles a toast to people who made it to the top. Smoke the right cigarette or drive the right car—so the ads imply—and girls will be swooning into your deodorized arms or caressing your expensive lapels. Happiness goes to the man who has the sweet smell of achievement. He is our national idol, and everybody else is our national fink.

I want to put in a word for the fink, especially the teen-age fink, because if we give him time to get through his finkdom—if we release him from the pressure of attaining certain goals by a certain age—he has a good chance of becoming our national idol, a Jefferson or a Thoreau, a Buckminster Fuller or an Adlai Stevenson, a man with a mind of his own. We need mavericks and dissenters and dreamers far more than we need junior vice-presidents. but we paralyze them by insisting that every step be a step up to the next rung of the ladder. Yet in the fluid years of youth, the only way for boys and girls to find their proper road is often to take a hundred side trips, poking out in different directions, faltering, drawing back, and starting again.

"But what if we fail?" they ask, whispering the dreadful word across the Generation Gap to their parents, who are back home at the Establishment, nursing their "middle-class values" and cultivating their "goal-oriented society." The parents whisper back: "Don't!"

What they should say is "Don't be afraid to fail!" Failure isn't fatal. Countless people have had a bout with it and come out stronger as a result. Many have even come out famous. History is strewn with eminent dropouts, "loners" who followed their own trail, not worrying about its odd twists and turns because they had faith in their own sense of direction. To read their biographies is always exhilarating, not only because they beat the system, but because their system was better than the one that they beat.

Luckily, such rebels still turn up often enough to prove that individualism, though badly threatened, is not extinct. Much has been written, for instance, about the fitful scholastic career of Thomas P. F. Hoving, New York's former Parks Commissioner and now director of the Metropolitan Museum of Art. Hoving was a dropout's dropout, entering and leaving schools as if they were motels, often at the request of the management. Still, he must have learned something during those unorthodox years, for he dropped in again at the top of his profession.

His case reminds me of another boyhood—that of Holden Caulfield in J. D. Salinger's *The Catcher in the Rye,* the most popular literary hero of the postwar period. There is nothing accidental about the grip that this dropout continues to hold on the affections of an entire American generation. Nobody else, real or invented, has made such an engaging shambles of our "goal-oriented society," so gratified our secret belief that the "phonies" are in power and the good guys up the creek. Whether Holden has also reached the top of his chosen field today is one of those speculations that delight fanciers of good fiction. I speculate that he has. Holden Caulfield, incidentally, is now thirty-six.

I'm not urging everyone to go out and fail just for the sheer therapy of it, or to quit college just to coddle some vague discontent. Obviously it's better to succeed than to flop, and in general a long education is more helpful than a short one. (Thanks to my own education, for example, I can tell George Eliot from T. S. Eliot, I can handle the pluperfect tense in French, and I know that

Caesar beat the Helvetii because he had enough frumentum.) I only mean that failure isn't bad in itself, or success automatically good.

Fred Zinnemann, who has directed some of Hollywood's most honored movies, was asked by a reporter, when *A Man for All Seasons* won every prize, about his previous film, *Behold a Pale Horse,* which was a box-office disaster. "I don't feel any obligation to be successful," Zinnemann replied. "Success can be dangerous—you feel you know it all. I've learned a great deal from my failures." A similar point was made by Richard Brooks about his ambitious money loser, *Lord Jim.* Recalling the three years of his life that went into it, talking almost with elation about the troubles that befell his unit in Cambodia, Brooks told me that he learned more about his craft from this considerable failure than from his many earlier hits.

It's a point, of course, that applies throughout the arts. Writers, playwrights, painters and composers work in the expectation of periodic defeat, but they wouldn't keep going back into the arena if they thought it was the end of the world. It isn't the end of the world. For an artist—and perhaps for anybody—it is the only way to grow.

Today's younger generation seems to know that this is true, seems willing to take the risks in life that artists take in art. "Society," needless to say, still has the upper hand—it sets the goals and condemns as a failure everybody who won't play. But the dropouts and the hippies are not as afraid of failure as their parents and grandparents. This could mean, as their elders might say, that they are just plumb lazy, secure in the comforts of an affluent state. It could also mean, however, that they just don't buy the old standards of success and are rapidly writing new ones.

Recently it was announced, for instance, that more than two hundred thousand Americans have inquired about service in VISTA (the domestic Peace Corps) and that, according to a Gallup survey, "more than 3 million American college students would serve VISTA in some capacity if given the opportunity." This is hardly the road to riches or to an executive suite. Yet I have met many of these young volunteers, and they are not pining for traditional success. On the contrary, they appear more fulfilled than the average vice-president with a swimming pool.

Who is to say, then, if there is any right path to the top, or even to say what the top consists of? Obviously the colleges don't have more than a partial answer—otherwise the young would not be so disaffected with an education that they consider vapid. Obviously business does not have the answer—otherwise the young would not be so scornful of its call to be an organization man.

The fact is, nobody has the answer, and the dawning awareness of this fact seems to me one of the best things happening in America today. Success and failure are again becoming individual visions, as they were when the country was younger, not rigid categories. Maybe we are learning again to cherish this right of every person to succeed on his own terms and to fail as often as necessary along the way.

Goodbye (Whoosh) Forever

THERE'S GOOD NEWS in the paper: America has its first drive-in funeral parlor. I had almost given up hope that the country could reach the goal that it is so obviously striving for—the day when we will be able to do everything without getting out of the car. Now I know that the impossible dream is possible.

"Folks will be able just to drive by and view the last remains of their loved ones, and then keep going," said Hirschel Thornton, an Atlanta undertaker, explaining his newly opened "moratorium," which has five plate glass windows where the deceased can be exhibited to any motorist who wants to say good-bye. This is one of the human encounters, this final farewell, that I thought could never be conducted from an automobile. That's why Thornton's breakthrough is so thrilling. It recognizes that Americans want nothing so much as to "keep going"; yet it sees that the amenities are served. Surely no other society has made so brilliant a distinction between the quick and the dead.

I wouldn't be surprised if folks started moving to Atlanta just to die and spend a few days at Thornton's drive-in as a kindness to their friends. Bereaved relatives would be able to motor past at a respectable speed (anything over 20 mph would probably be insensitive), give a sincere wave to good old Harry, and keep going—perhaps to a drive-in bank to cash a check, then to a drive-through store to buy some food for breakfast, and on to a drive-in movie. It would make for a kicky couple of hours—so wonderfully American!—and, best of all, think of the pleasure it would give to good old Harry. He died modern and saved his friends a little time.

With this problem solved, the other social courtesies should be easy. Certainly, for instance, if a fleeting glance is honor enough for the newly dead, it's enough for the newly alive—the infants who have just been born. After all, they're going to be around for years; why waste a half hour parking the car and walking to the maternity ward and peering at them through the glass? They all look alike anyway. How much more efficient just to drive by in the car and give the kid a friendly honk.

As a matter of fact, it would be an ideal way to visit all hospital patients, young or old. Does a sick wife want her husband sitting at the bedside telling her that he loves her and that she looks fine, when she knows she looks awful? Surely such solace and affection don't do any good. I, for one, think she would recover much faster if she could see him driving by, during visitors' hours, behind the wheel of his car where he wants to be, happy and fulfilled. That's what marriage is all about.

And speaking of marriage, why not get the wedding ceremony out of church and into the car? If there can be drive-in movies, there can be drive-in weddings. The groom would wait at the altar in his convertible, the bride and her father would drive up in their convertible (preferably white), the minister would perform the ceremony standing up in *his* convertible, and at the words "I do" all of us guests would blow our horns. That should be ample proof to the young couple that we wish them well and that we'd like to be on our way. But if they want to take a few minutes more and form their cars into a receiving line, we can drive past.

Then all that remains is to get the other sacraments out of church. Here again my attitude has been old-fashioned, almost stick-in-the-mud. I've always thought that the worship of God was the ultimate private transaction, one requiring stillness of body and soul. But Thornton's drive-in mortuary has made me see that this is stale theology in the America of 1970. If God lives, He lives by the side of the road, for that's where His people are, and that's where we must seek Him. Let's tear down the churches and make them into little glass booths along our streets and highways, where priests and ministers can be exhibited praying. Folks will be able just to drive by and see their clergymen in reverent positions, and then keep going. Groovy!

Farewell to Shuffleboard

IT IS NOT NECESSARY to be a student of watersheds—though I happen to have a nice collection myself—to see that this is a watershed year for travel. A new age has abruptly begun, an old age has abruptly ended, and the whole business of crossing the ocean will never be the same again.

As in any decent watershed year, we have a conjunction of two events, one pointing to the future, one sealing off the past. The first is the advent of Boeing's 747 jet, a plane big enough to hold 490 passengers and 111 feet longer than the Wright Brothers' first flight. The other is the sudden retirement of the *United States,* flagship of America's fleet, for lack of customers. Laid up at a pier in the South, she joins five other idle American liners that also had proud names—*Independence*! *Con-*

stitution!—and proud histories. Together the six ships used to take 150,000 people a year to Europe and back, when much of the Atlantic traffic went by sea. Now it's 5 percent.

Obviously, in short, the 747 jet is the world's new ocean liner. And just as obviously that's how the airlines are trying to promote it, or her. Their ads ask us to imagine a spacious cruise ship where jolly people will walk and mingle. Thus they invoke as a nostalgic idea what they helped to destroy as a fact, implying that they will make every effort to duplicate aloft the fun that was shipboard life.

The only trouble is that shipboard life was never that much fun. In fact, if the truth were known—and it were —the jumbo jets can't be wholly blamed for putting ocean liners out of business. The passenger ships also killed themselves off by trying to entertain their passengers.

In all of travel there was no sight more depressing than the daily schedule that was slipped quietly—but never quietly enough—under the stateroom door at dawn, and no feat was more strenuous than trying to avoid the activities listed on it. I'm as sorry as the next man to lose the great gift that transatlantic liners could bestow: a relaxing of life's pace and a removal from its cares. But I've had my last Captain's Gala, and the next man is cowering under his steamer blanket to keep from being dragooned into a tango contest.

So when we weep for the ocean queens, let us not shed tears for the wrong reason. What we are giving up is a method of transportation that had beauty and leisure—reason enough to weep in this fretful age. But let's not pretend that we are giving up a wonderful social event.

Unless deck tennis is a wonderful social event. Or bouillon a wonderful drink.

No form of entertainment except possibly a Kabuki dance was frozen into so rigid a pattern for so long. The sins that were visited on couples crossing the Atlantic in the 1890s were visited on their sons and grandsons right through the 1960s. Monday night it was bingo, Tuesday its twin brother, horse racing. On Wednesday it was bingo and on Thursday horse racing. No new idea ever crossed the threshold of the Grand Salon, or any other salon.

Who, crossing the ocean for the first time, could have conceived in advance of treats so relentlessly banal? Did anyone prepare these novice travelers for their first glimpse of the ship's library, the place where old Edna Ferber novels go to die? Did anyone tell them about the two sloping Ping-Pong tables with only one ball, or the shuffleboard court with its markings worn off? Or the string trio playing gems from *Roberta*? Or the costume party? Or the ship's photographer snapping his comical pictures of the passengers at play?

Did anyone warn them about the Captain's Gala on the last night out, that bubbly pledging of eternal friendship by people in paper hats who will never see each other again? Prodded by that tireless guru, the social director, they gamely try to pass an orange around the dance floor without using their hands. Happiness, they have been told, is right under their nose if they will only look for it, and for this one brief moment they will even look under their chin. Like the orange, however, it tends to roll away.

Therefore the world's airlines, poised on a new era of mass transport, should think twice—if at all—about trying to divert their passengers. Technically, of course, it would be easy to make the 747 look like an ocean liner. Deck chairs could be placed around the perimeter of the giant cabin, leaving room on the outside for strollers to stroll and for bores to bore, and on the inside for Ping-Pong, bingo and bridge.

But all that we really want from the 747 is to get there in reasonable comfort and to be left alone—which is what we always wanted from the ocean liners and never got. Give us the little talk about the oxygen mask that will drop down in case whatever it is that happens to the cabin pressure happens ("Simply clamp over mouth"). Demonstrate the life jacket that can be inflated by any of three methods, none of them comprehensible ("Simply pull the red toggle pins outward in a clockwise direction"). Tell us how to dial the nine channels of music selected for our listening pleasure from Respighi to Rod McKuen ("Simply plug in ears"). Tell us the stuff about the air speed and the ground speed and the "slight turbulence" that's expected at the strato-cumulus cloud layer. Give us food and drink and something to read, and maybe a movie, and a pillow to hasten sleep. Then seal the pilot's lips with tape. For if sleep comes, the metallic crackle of his voice will not be far behind, jolting us from slumber to see an unusually good view of Bangor out the left window.

Perhaps we should want it to be otherwise. As the number of our fellow passengers increases, so should our ability to enjoy their company and to feel a little less alone. Yet when all is said (by the pilot) and done (by the stewardess), flight is still a solitary encounter with our own emotions. Nothing can quite rid us of the vestigial feeling that we are creatures of the ground and ought never to have left it, and there are moments, as our jet makes endless droning circles in a holding pattern, when we wonder if we can hold our nerves in a pattern as steady as the plane's.

At such times the pilot might well think that a game of shuffleboard would help, or a Pilot's Gala the last hour out. It wouldn't.

Commencement Address

MEMBERS OF THE graduating class of Fenton University:

Today it is my honor as commencement speaker to send you forth onto the turbulent seas of life. My only regret is that your president—my esteemed friend George Thurlow—cannot be here to share this proud moment with you. I am told that President Thurlow is now entering his third week in Room 304 of Hodgkins Hall as a hostage of the ad hoc Committee to Define Radical Alternatives. How we shall miss the sage words of counsel which he assuredly would have wished to impart to the Class of 1968 as you bid farewell to the ivied groves of Academe!

Nor can I conceal my disappointment that your distinguished Board of Trustees also cannot be here—the first time in the hallowed 122-year history of Fenton, I believe, that they have failed to lend their august presence to the graduation ceremony. I can only defer to their judgment that it was more important to attend the meeting called by the student-faculty steering committee for the Gradual Elimination of Trustees (GET) in order to seek common ground on this substantive issue.

Indeed, as I gaze out across your ranks, I am struck by how sparsely your class appears to be represented at its own graduation. Some of your number, I realize, are in detention—I think Chief Muldoon said the total came to thirty-six—as a result of the New Left Alliance "smoke-in" last night at "Old North" which so regrettably got out of control. It is hard to believe that those stately Greek columns will no longer stand sentinel over Fraternity Row.

Nor should I blame, I suppose, the several hundred members of your class who went home on March seventeenth when studies were so abruptly terminated—never, alas, to be resumed. What a pity it is that the administration has not yet found it possible to meet all thirty-one demands of the Student Protest Coordinating Committee for "a searching new look at the university's decision-making process."

I have just been handed a note from Provost Hockaday, who asks me to make the following announcement: "If there are any students here from the Che Guevara chapter of the Students for a Participatory Democracy (SAPD) who are authorized to negotiate with the faculty Subcommittee of Five for withdrawal from the Consortium of Orbital Ballistic Research (COBR) will they please go at once to the implosion room of Greeley Physics Lab?" Thank you. Quite a few of you, I see. Well, these are busy times.

Indeed, I noticed that a number of your class left a

few minutes ago during the presentation of an honorary degree—Doctor of Humane Letters, as I recall—to your eminent alumnus L. Fred Potter '08, "grand old man of American free enterprise." How ironic! For as I listened to that stirring citation, as I looked at that stern yet kindly visage beneath locks whitened by half a century of honest toil, I could not but reflect that the mortal journey of L. F. Potter is a living storybook of the very virtues which I had hoped to commend to you today, my young friends, as you set out upon your holy quest for the American dream. Starting as a poor pharmacist in Sandusky, Ohio, he never flagged in his vision of an industrial empire that would hurl back the frontiers of ignorance and darkness. And I know whereof I speak, for it was his company that developed Maim, the riot repellent which proved so effective at my own alma mater, Bidwell, during the recent fracas between the Majority Coalition and the "jock faction" over the building of a community bowling alley.

This morning, however, the torch passes to you, and I say grasp it proudly. Grasp proudly and hold high the eternal flame of learning which from the age of Socrates has illumined man's inextinguishable . . . Can you hear me? Those explosions from the ROTC building are most annoying. I'll try to talk louder. GRASP PROUDLY AND HOLD HIGH THE ETERNAL FL—

Thank you, young lady. This seems to be a note from President Thurlow. He evidently dropped it from the window of 304 Hodgkins Hall to a coed representing one of the student counterinsurgent groups. As it is George Thurlow's first word to the outside in fifteen days, I shall read it without delay:

"This is a message from your president. First, I want to say this—and let me make myself perfectly clear: I shall never mitigate my efforts toward collective determinations to restructure the infrastructure of the university—always in parallel, of course, with the paraconstitutional concerns of legitimized authority. Second, I want to say this: bring me back my cigars."

I'm sure we all wish President Thurlow a swift recovery of his "pernicious weed."

New sons of Fenton! We are gathered one final time under these noble elms to solemnize an important moment for each of you. Today you leave the quiet shelter of a college campus for a world where life will no longer be tidy. On the contrary, you will meet disorder and even ferment. How fitting, therefore, is this traditional rite of severing the old and "commencing" the new.

Some of you, perhaps, question its relevance. We need only glance at the banner, GRADUATIONS ARE FUNKY, which I take to be a term of opprobrium, hanging virtually over my head from the balcony of Glover Administration Building—still held, I gather, by units of Students Alienated from a Sick Society (SASS) —to be reminded that there no longer exists a unanimity on this point.

In fact, I am informed by Acting President Butterwick —whom we are so fortunate to have with us, as he is the sole representative of the administration and the faculty —that no fewer than four dissident graduations are currently being held in various centers of student activity, including one in the ever popular Peking Bar & Grill across from Findley Gate. Indeed, I wonder if I might have a show of hands: how many members of Fenton's graduating class still remain in my audience? Only one? I see. Apparently the ad hoc Commencement Coordinating Committee did not avail in its last-hour "appeal for unity."

So it is to you, then, young man, that I address my thoughts on this felicitous occasion. For was it not said by the poet that if but one candle flickereth in the long night of mankind, it will cast a glow bright enough to . . . You're leaving too? No doubt duty calls you, also, to a meeting of some sort. These old eyes can't quite read that placard you are carrying.

Well, Godspeed, young man. And to the rest of you, parents and friends of this distinguished graduating class, I can only say . . . Good heavens! Was that a bomb? . . . I can only say that this concludes the 122nd commencement exercises of Fenton University.

Thank you.

The Memoir Bore

MY WIFE SAYS that I'm a "memoir bore," and it's true. I collar every old person who tells me an even remotely interesting story of his past—usually involving some vanished way of life—and plead with him to write it.

"Why should I?" my victims ask. "Who would care?"

I tell them to write it for their children, or for their grandchildren, or for the local historical society, or just for themselves—anything to get it down. I've seen too much good family material and regional detail die with its last custodian.

Now, however, I can report that all is not dead in Memory Lane. I am at the Indiana University Writers' Conference, one of the best known of the workshops for aspiring writers that bloom so profusely across America every summer. I'm here to teach nonfiction to a group of men and women who have come from many corners of the country, each bringing some private dream of putting part of himself on paper and seeing his words in print.

The dream is a common one—who doesn't think he would like to "try a little writing sometime"?—and I have often wondered what kind of people attend these conferences. I expected the ones at Indiana to be fairly young: boys and girls not long out of college, or still in college, poised on new frontiers of expression, needing only a final push. Therefore when the manuscripts of the twenty-five students who had qualified for my class arrived by mail, I looked at them eagerly to see what the opening sentences were like. They were like this:

"Parsons Junction at the turn of the century was only a village. I can still remember walking to Wallace's Ice Cream Parlor, where 'Doc' Wallace . . ."

"Probably it was crazy for a pair of newlyweds at the start of the Depression to think they could just climb into an old jalopy and . . ."

"Standing in my undershorts at the induction center, a kid from Nebraska going off to fight the Kaiser, I thought back to all the . . ."

Obviously my boys and girls were longer out of college than any of us would have liked. Obviously, too, the job would not be to point them toward the future, but to harness what they remembered of the past. For what they were remembering was an America that does not exist today except in the minds of those who were there.

I meet my twenty-five students every morning for an hour. The majority are women, and on the whole they are between forty and sixty-five, their children grown up, their main career over. Their faces, however, are attentive and lively. Quite a few have had articles published in a farm journal or a church magazine, or in the

Sunday supplement of their paper. But none of them is a writer; they are just people who have taken up writing.

The class is also audited by men and women who are registered in some other workshop—the novel or the short story, the children's book or the poem or the play. There are 125 students altogether, and they scurry between the different sessions, avid for every last secret of success. It is rather like a ship's cruise, for we are bound on a common voyage, kept busy day and night, seldom getting out of the building where we are quartered—an immense complex of rooms that serve almost every human need. When we arrived, the sign outside said WELCOME WRITERS! After three days it was changed, and now it says TRY BOWLING! Perhaps the real point of a writers' conference comes down to that: to help the natural writers to write and the natural bowlers to find some other dream.

This happens partly in class. There is only so much, however, that can be taught about writing, and the real transaction, if it occurs, is a private one. Every student is entitled to a half hour with the teacher to discuss his manuscript. But the sessions often stretch to an hour, or are resumed at odd moments through the week—in the cafeteria at breakfast, in the lounge at night. For that's when we can finally get past the "writer" and his manuscript to the more important question—who he is as a person and what he wants to say.

Not all my students want to be antiquarians. Some have submitted topical humor, generally the humor of domestic mishap or of a mother bemused by a teen-age son. Some have written travel books about the place where they have gone to retire. But most, being of a certain age when they start to write, write about the past. Not that anything dramatic happened in their lives; on the contrary, the appeal of these stories is that we can see ourselves in most of them.

There is the 1931 newlywed, for instance, who went into the mountains of Tennessee with her husband, built a crude cabin, and survived on a margin of food and hope which, now, seems hopelessly thin. What she learned about life from her neighbors, and from within herself, is everybody's experience of the Depression, yet it is not quite anyone else's.

There is the woman who remembers the fictitious radio characters of the thirties as clearly as if they were her college roommates. She remembers them because they were the people she invested with reality, real life being too bleak. It is the Depression seen through another lens.

There is the woman who recalls how her father, a poor country doctor, allowed his patients to pay their bill with products which weren't much good, but which he valued on a scale that had nothing to do with money.

There is the man who grew up in the town that Edgar Lee Masters left and later embittered by writing *Spoon River Anthology.* This man eventually went to New York himself, got to know Masters, and found that the pain can be as sharp for those who cut their Midwestern ties as for those who stay behind.

Such material—and it's typical—can't help depressing the small number of young people who are at the conference. For obviously one problem that must be faced in class is the special problem of writing reminiscence: how to extract, from the dreary mass of total recall, the few elements that have meaning beyond one particular life and one particular town.

Still, I see no point in trying to modernize the old. Why deflect them from the subject they know best? True, their memoirs often appear to be mere nostalgia, mere longing for a simpler age. But I think these men and women are also looking back in order to find—and to fix in writing—values which they once believed were true and which gave the country its continuity.

Today who can blame them if they feel that all continuity has fled? American families have never been so fragmented, children have never known so little about where their parents and grandparents grew up. We are also a society on the move, shifted with such frequency by big corporations that husbands and wives no longer say "We're Iowa people" or "We're from New England." They say "We're General Electric people" or "We're Union Carbide people." What kind of people is that? Are we really beginning to lose our sense of who we are and where we came from?

These are the roots that my new friends at Indiana have gone in search of. As a teacher of writing I wish they were better writers. But as a memoir bore I've never had it so good.

Annual Report of The National Refractory & Brake Company

TO OUR STOCKHOLDERS

1969 was a year of adjustment for your company.

The general slowdown in the American economy resulted in a softening of demand for the products of the National Refractory & Brake Company and a consequent reduction in worldwide unit sales. Unexpectedly high start-up costs were also incurred—notably, in the prototype development of sophisticated capacitors—which contributed to a marked reversal of anticipated gains in 1969.

On balance, however, it was a year of progress. Strong product line in several of your company's new divisions —i.e., anhydrous petrochemicals—found public acceptance indicating significant movement toward profitability. Nor should we minimize the generally healthy performance of the Wholesale Price Index and the decreasing scarcity of Euro-Dollars.

Nevertheless your management concerted its efforts during 1969 on a realignment of production facilities to increase peak-day delivery capacity and to optimize negative factors occurring in the inventory accumulation program. Earnings for the year were $68,412,677, or $1.50 per share, down approximately 31% from $98,612,409, or $2.17 per share, in 1968.

EXECUTIVE RESTRUCTURING

Major changes in the executive structure of National Refractory & Brake were effected during the fourth quarter when it was realized that greater top-management depth and flexibility would be required to meet the sharp competitive challenges of the future.

Roger S. Bassinger, who became chairman and chief executive officer on January 12, 1969, resigned on October 3, 1969, for reasons of health. His resignation was accepted with an expression of appreciation for his services to the company, which he joined in 1932 as a flocculating technician. At the same time, Carl M. Baxter, president, and Victor L. Morrissey, Jr., executive vice-president for production and finance, were appointed to newly created posts in Gabon and Malaysia, respectively, where they will explore long-term development opportunities for your company in the emerging nations.

The restructuring of top authority calls for a seven-man Corporate Executive Group headed by Harley G. Waller, who became chairman upon the resignation of Mr. Bassinger. They will oversee 12 senior vice-presidents and 22 junior vice-presidents at the division and development level. Your management is confident that this realignment will provide greater vertical integration and enable N.R. & B. to overcome underutilization of capacity.

Edgar J. Barton remains as president and chief operating officer of the Barton Brake Company, which became a wholly-owned subsidiary in 1959 and which continues to be the sole component to show a profit.

LABOR SITUATION

Minor work stoppages had an adverse effect on earnings in 1969. These included the 51-day shutdown by the Propulsion Workers' Union at our fossil fuels plant in Schenectady; the three-week strike at our Huntsville facility, which halted production of fluidic devices for the Castor & Pollux "space twin" project; the 91-day stoppage in the Oxacrylic® Sta-Glo® division at Bayonne, N.J., where we had already experienced substantial pre-operational and break-in costs, and the "sit-in" by the Brotherhood of Button Installers at our thermal underwear plant in Bismarck, N.D., which began on May 4 and which, regrettably, has not been resolved as of this writing.

On balance, however, your management believes that its relations with the labor community are among the most harmonious in American industry. With only scattered exceptions, the 31 other work stoppages against the company were settled in seven days or less and generally without violence. We need only mention the "birthday package" negotiated by Mr. Bassinger with the drill punch operators at Cocoa Beach, Fla., whereby each member of the union will receive a day off for his own birthday and the birthday of two other dependent relatives. The full impact of these payroll costs began to be felt shortly before Mr. Bassinger's resignation as chairman.

RESEARCH AND DEVELOPMENT

Your company is a staunch believer in progress. We have always maintained as our credo that a stronger America is a stronger National Refractory & Brake. Accordingly, your management made sizable capital investments in plant and equipment during 1969 to meet projected demands from the aerospace and nucleonics industries.

Typical of these investments was the construction of a prototype filter house on Guam to convert ordinary kelp into vinyl foam for lining the interior of Vulcan II "Mars probe" missiles. This very complex process continues to raise costly problems, and the plant was placed in standby condition in April while engineers studied modifications required to compensate for the failure of the reactor to react.

Preliminary results of the study, issued on September 22, cast considerable doubt on the feasibility of converting kelp into vinyl foam. They did, however, indicate a significant likelihood of converting vinyl foam into kelp, and a full-scale analysis of the international kelp market was consequently initiated. As of December, owing to uncertainties of the monetary situation in Southeast Asia, there was reported to be "little or no demand for kelp." Meanwhile, the Guam facility will remain in standby condition and feasibility studies for its use will be continued.

Similar difficulties in the shakedown phase of several other divisions occurred during 1969—typically, the incident involving our Computer Software Division in its development of a memory module for passenger trains. This module, designed to replace the crew of a train, offered major savings to railroad managements in this age of mounting operational costs and outrageous labor demands, and we were gratified by the decision of the New Haven Railroad to test it on a commuter run from Westport to New York on September 11. It is to be regretted that the memory module apparently lost its memory capacity and took the passengers to Providence, R.I., where they were given lunch at company expense and returned to their homes by bus. The resultant adverse publicity, while naturally disappointing, had the favorable effect of redoubling our determination to unlock the secrets of microelectronic circuitry.

On balance, however, it was a year of progress, and the development by the Barton Brake Company of a nonslip bicycle brake was widely hailed by the transportation and recreation trades.

SAFETY

Protection of life and limb has always been a watchword to your company. National Refractory's safety record for 1969 showed an injury frequency of 3.26 per million man-hours worked, compared to 1.83 in 1968. The slight increase can be traced to our vanitory surfacing plant in Davenport, Iowa, where the auditorium ceiling collapsed and fell during the showing of two training films, *Watch Those Fingers!* and *Heads Up!*

LITIGATION

On June 11, 1969, the Fifth District Court found National Refractory & Brake in restraint of trade with respect to its Shoo-Fly® line of systemic pesticides. The complainant was the manufacturer of Roach-Off, a competitive product, and your company was found guilty on two counts of violating the "little Sherman Act" and of conspiracy to avoid the Smoot-Wadley provision.

Your company is convinced that the decision is wrong and we are vigorously pursuing every course to have it corrected. Should the judgment be upheld by the Second Court of Appeals, it is counsel's opinion that we will be faced with treble damage suits. Eighteen such suits are now pending and more may be expected. As of this writing, no legal means of meeting the cost of these suits can be envisioned by your company in view of the indebtedness already incurred as a result of adverse factors previously cited in this report.

Your management's long relationship with Horton, Horton & Bird, general counsel, was terminated on June 12, 1969.

INTERNATIONAL OPERATIONS

1969 was a year of transition for many of the foreign nations in which National Refractory & Brake operates. The outbreak of hostilities, for example, among the Trucial Sheikdoms of the Middle East, where we had struck rich deposits of epoxy, coupled with the threatened closure of the Persian Gulf and the sporadic harassment of pipelines by Arab nationalists, reduced our output at this overseas affiliate in 1969 to 27 bbls.

Currency instabilities in many other countries—i.e., the sudden fluctuation, unanticipated by your treasurer, of the dinar, the rupia, the piaster and the Straits Dollar —necessitated the borrowing of $38,000,000 from the Bank of Zurich at 7½% for future sinking fund requirements. Arrangements for revolving credits of $19,000,000 from the International Coin Fund in Geneva were also sought in an airmail letter dated August 28, 1969. No reply, however, has been received to date.

On the positive side, the Barton Brake Company found overwhelming acceptance of its Euro-Brakes, a product specially tooled to the metric requirements of the "Inner Seven" countries. Brake sales by the Barton subsidiary in 1969 reached an all-time high in 72 overseas markets, contributing importantly to the division's net profit for the year of $3,981,012.

FUTURE OUTLOOK

There come times in the life of any corporation when management must candidly appraise its viability in the face of ever-increasing competition, high start-up costs for new breeder technologies, and uncertainties in the world political and monetary situation, coupled with the mounting and often unreasonable demands of organized labor and the decreasing availability of top executive talent due to the apparent reluctance of American youth to enter business as a career. In the foregoing Annual Report we have attempted to make such an appraisal, hoping that it will clarify a question frequently asked by our stockholders, namely, why National Refractory & Brake has paid no dividend since the third quarter of 1962.

In this connection it is our duty to announce that your company has received an attractive offer of purchase. The prospective purchaser is the Barton Brake Company. We are advised that Mr. Barton is in the process of forming a conglomerate corporation, to be named General United Allied Affiliated, and that he has also issued tenders to such diversified firms as Titan Films, Trans-Sky Airlines, the Trenton "News-Intelligencer," Full o' Pep Breakfast Cereals, and the Honolulu "Mets."

The proposed corporation, while seemingly unrelated in its component units, would afford the Barton interests a strong position in the consumer fields of entertainment, transportation, communications, food and sports, to which the purchase of National Refractory & Brake would add a broad spectrum of sophisticated software systems. The manufacture of refractories would in all likelihood be discontinued and the name of your company changed to Barton & Sons. Interestingly, this would appear to be the first instance of a parent firm being purchased by one of its own subsidiaries. Whether present management would be retained is a matter of continuing interest to the officers of your company.

The Barton offer, now under intensive study by the SEC, the FAA, the FDA, the CIA, the PTA and the Second Court of Appeals, is for 51% of National Refractory common stock outstanding, at $3.15 per share. On the day of the offer, February 2, 1970, the stock was trading at 11¼. While this bid may appear to be appreciably lower than market price, your management considers itself fortunate to have found a solution to the hitherto insuperable problems of its sizable noncurrent indebtedness, its $38,000,000 loan from the Bank of Zurich, its probable damages resulting from the pesticide suits, its inoperative kelp facility on Guam, its projected payroll costs in excess of projected capital, its inability to adjust to international monetary fluctuations, and other difficulties too numerous to mention in this brief report.

For the Board of Directors

Harley G. Waller
CHAIRMAN

March 3, 1970

An Apple a Day Keeps the Flexowriter Away

IF YOU SOMETIMES FEEL that the human element is going out of the practice of medicine in this country—a feeling which, I'll admit, probably isn't shared by more than 85 percent of the population—you might consider moving to the Bensonhurst section of Brooklyn, where, according to the *New York Times,* a new medical center will enable its doctors and dentists to offer "automated cordiality."

"The cheery personal word that will make the form letter seem not so much like a form letter—'How is Andy's hernia?' or 'Tell your Grandma she left her galoshes'—will be passed to a typist by the physician," says the *Times.* "The typist will insert the homey touch in the appropriate place as the Friden automatic programmed 'Flexowriter' rattles off the form letters requesting payment for the last visit or informing that the

X-rays of the patient (kidney) (arm) (stomach) (chest) came out negative."

Well, heaven knows I always appreciate a cheery personal word from the doctor—come to think of it, mine hasn't asked about Andy's hernia for several years—but still I'd rather have a doctor send no word at all than turn the writing over to a Flexowriter. For obviously, if I read the *Times* story correctly—always a possibility—he is using the Flexowriter as more than a scribe. He is also letting it decide, in a multiple-choice question, which part of me (kidney) (arm) (stomach) (chest) is sick.

This sort of thing can't help making people feel that the American doctor is just too busy. Most of us are apprehensive enough already. It's no fun to call our general practitioner and not have him remember what ails us, what he last prescribed, or even who we are. It's easy enough for him to remember Grandma—she keeps leaving her galoshes in the waiting room. Besides, even a Flexowriter would be fairly safe in diagnosing her trouble as (senility) (hardening of arteries) (failing vision) (doesn't like galoshes).

But what about the rest of us? Can we really afford to narrow our illnesses down to (kidney) (arm) (stomach) (chest) just to help the doctor unload some work onto a computer of limited diagnostic range? Surely in this anxious age we are entitled to a more multiple choice of ailments. What about that throbbing in my (temple) (eyes) (sinuses), that ringing in my (head) (ears) (telephone), that tennis elbow on my (elbow) and housemaid's knee on my (housemaid)?

In all fairness, I should point out that the doctor doesn't let the Flexowriter give any bad news about the X-rays. It is only programmed to say that they came out negative, which evidently is good news—or so I have assumed, at least, since 1937, when "Dizzy" Dean was felled by a baseball and doctors later reported that "X-rays of Dean's head showed nothing." Flexowriter, in fact, is not even permitted to stroke its chin in reasonable doubt. It isn't programmed, for instance, to say that "the X-rays came out (negative) (positive) (blurry)."

Still, I foresee many a slip between the typist and the computer as she tries to "insert the homey touch in the appropriate place as the . . . Flexowriter rattles off the form letters requesting payment." How will she know—to take the most obvious pitfall—which is the homey touch? Is it Andy's hernia, or is it the request for payment? Will she know what the appropriate place is? *Is* there an appropriate place for a homey touch in a form letter? Will the Flexowriter be rattling along so fast that she just has to throw the homey touch in anywhere? Or will the machine itself boggle at the task of sorting the medical items from the cheery personal words? Cordiality could well be automated to come out like this:

DEAR PATIENT:

You'll be amused to hear that you left your (kidney) (arm) (stomach) (chest) in my office last week. We'll put it in a safe place and you can drop by for it whenever you're "out our way."

On a more serious note, I'm pleased to be able to inform you that the X-rays of your grandma's galoshes came out negative. Therefore in my judgment it will not be necessary to operate on them.

Incidentally, just for laughs, would you tell your mother—great gal!—that she still owes me $75 for that consultation back in 1963 about possibly removing her (tonsils) (gall-bladder) (head)?

Very cordially,
DOCTOR

Ironically, though the individual doctor is dying out and the house call is almost as extinct as the (dodo) (passenger pigeon) (great auk), it does seem easy today to get physicians by the team. I'm thinking of all those magazine layouts in which platoons of surgeons, cardiologists, hematologists, anesthesiologists and biomedical engineers are clustered around the patient, plying him with laser knives, ultrasonic frequencies or radioactive albumin particles, freezing his tissues with cryosurgery or aerating his blood in hyperbaric tents, preventing his arrhythmias with defibrillating units or loosening his atherosclerosis deposits with jets of carbon dioxide. To read about such prodigies of medical teamwork is to take comfort against a darker day.

But somewhere between the cryosurgical brain probe, on the one hand, and, on the other, a form letter from Flexowriter prescribing two galoshes every four hours, stands mere Everyman with his hay fever and flat feet, his insomnia and shortening breath, his tired back and tired blood, his real or imagined messages of disarray from every gland and organ and his need to be assured, regularly, that science has an answer for them all.

I don't know where other people will find such steady assurance, but my own solution is to watch the Lawrence Welk show every Saturday night. In that halcyon land of Serutan and Sedalin and Bufferin and Q-Tips, of Sominex and Devarex and Geritol and Cope, the goddess Hygeia reigns even more supreme than she did in ancient Greece, promising balm for the acid digestive tract, the clogged intestine, the congested sinus, the frayed nerve, the pounding head, the bunioned toe, the slipping disc and the waxy ear, rejuvenating the old and drowsy, nudging the sleepless off to sleep.

Of course I don't watch Welk's part of the program—

only the commercials. That's the new mainstream of American medicine, right of Medicare and left of Saint Petersburg, and as for "homey touches," even Flexowriter can't beat it. If home is where you can hear the dentures clack at meal time and the bronchial tubes whistle through the night, Dr. Welk's clinic will make you feel right at home. He cares about your (corns) (gums) (post-nasal drip) (gas).

Peabody's Complaint

THIS IS ONE of those days when I almost wish I were not a literary critic. How can one hope in a brief book review to assess the merits—indeed, the incalculable influence—of a novel which dares, as *Peabody's Complaint* so brilliantly does, to shoulder the whole heavy burden of white Anglo-Saxon Protestant guilt and to reduce it at the end, with a comic flip of the wrist that would be hilarious if it were not so sad, to a mere bag of exploded myths? With this self-mocking yet strangely purgative journey into the WASP gestalt, author Winthrop Bradford has made it well-nigh impossible for other writers who deal in the upper-class Protestant milieu—one thinks of Louis Auchincloss—ever to work this territory again. *Peabody's Complaint,* which I am tempted to call a masterpiece, is the ultimate novel of the WASP's Puritan morality at war with the stirrings of a repressed libido.

Much, of course, has already been written about the book as a publishing "event": the $125,000 advance, the $175,000 paperback contract, the $250,000 sale to a motion picture company. There have also been reports—ever since two chapters appeared last year in *Boys' Life*—about the explicit language that the author uses to describe the erotic fancies of his protagonist, Goodhue Peabody, Jr. I can only say that the rumors are true; this reviewer, at least, has never seen the new permissiveness carried to such an extreme. Typical, perhaps, is the scene in which Peabody recalls being sent to dancing class at the age of ten and having an insatiable desire to pull off the white gloves of his partner, Dee-Dee Fahnestock:

> Finally I could control my hands no longer, and I still remember the frightened look in Dee-Dee's eyes when I took hold of her glove—it was the left one—and began to slide it off. I felt the soft satin yield beneath my fingers. Then, unaccountably, something stopped me. I wish I could say—for even today the memory fills me with a shame which is not, however, unmixed with lust—that it was my Puritan conscience tightening the rein on my unbridled id, as, God knows, it had so many times before and would again. But what actually stopped me was that I couldn't get the glove off because the damn thing went several inches above the elbow. Oh, the hot tears of frustration I shed that night for being born into a social class where the girls go muffled in organdy!

Permissive? Of course. There's no denying the initial shock of seeing words like "organdy" in print. But only a prude would question Bradford's artistic right to let his characters talk with such unflinching candor. For thereby he has found exactly the right tone, it seems to me, to express his own agonized search into the subsoil of American manners for the twisted root-causes of Protestant self-flagellation.

The plan of the book is simple. It takes place in the rectory of the Episcopal Church of Saint Edward the Confessor (a not unintended irony), and it consists of Peabody talking to his minister, the Reverend Amory S. T. Milbank, about the accumulated hang-ups of a lifetime. Or, I should say, the hang-ups of all the lifetimes of all his ancestors beginning with Increase Peabody, who landed at Plymouth in 1622, founded a bank, and was caught peeping at an Indian maiden bathing naked in a nearby stream. Thus Bradford establishes the twin themes which form Peabody's "complaint" and which, in a larger theological context of original sin, form the collective guilt of the Protestant Episcopal manchild: namely, his remorse over making so much money and his carnal yen for girls of a lower and therefore untouchable caste.

"Tell me, Reverend Milbank," Peabody asks the rector in a burst of self-revelation that may offend some readers with its frankness, "what is this compulsion that we have for banking? As early as nine years old I would lock myself in my room—three or four times a day—and do compound interest. Sometimes I even did it during dinner. Once I excused myself from the family table, saying I felt sick, and went into the bathroom and figured the compound interest on the Rockefeller estate at 4¼ percent for twenty years. My mother, who was a Lowell, kept knocking very politely on the door. 'What on earth are you doing in there for so long, Goody, dear?' she called. 'Please come out—your father wants to read us all something from *The Wall Street Journal.*' How could I tell her what I was doing? Or that I couldn't stop doing it?"

It is an episode that recurs over and over, well into Peabody's teens. The locale may change—it might be the lavatory of the Buckley School, for instance, or under the bath houses at the Piping Rock Club—but the obsession is always the same, and one can only admire Bradford's integrity for confronting such a long-hidden taboo so openly. With this giant leap of the imagination he has pushed the literature of Protestant adolescence far beyond Penrod and the Hardy Boys.

Equally courageous is his handling of the novel's other theme, the hitherto forbidden subject of Indian sex. True, I was shocked at the first mention of it, when Peabody comes right out and says, "Let's face it, Dr. Milbank, I have a thing about Indian girls, especially Iroquois." But then I realized that only by this very act of spoken expiation—by moving out, as it were, beyond guilt—could Peabody exorcise the buried fears and fantasies that had made him psychologically impotent, stunted by the Freudian dread of tribal castration.

Nor does he stop with mere words. Driven by the need to find some meaning in his aberrant sexual bent, he tracks down the diaries of his ancestors and finds that the taint did not end with Increase Peabody, but descended in a direct line through his son Cotton, his grandson Enoch, and his great-grandsons Caleb and Jonathan. No wonder Goodhue Peabody, Jr., the vessel for three and a half centuries of bottled-up lechery, decides to "get it out once and for all." And what an uproarious romp it is, leading him to an Iroquois reservation where, one night in a tepee with six Indian girls dressed only in beads, half blind with firewater and desire, he gives himself to a bizarre form of the ancient "potlatch" ceremony, emerging three days later with a gigantic hangover but oddly purified. "I've had it with the Indian broads," he tells the Reverend Milbank in the rectory over tea.

Yet Bradford is too good a writer to let us off as easily as that. At the end we are left with the knowledge that Peabody's voyage through the dark night of the soul is but one of many that he will be called upon to make, and it is this rare insight into the human condition which raises the novel to grandeur. I, at least, found myself curiously moved by the possibilities of both pain and hope adumbrated in the final question that Peabody puts to the minister: "Say, do you think I've got any chance of making out with a Jewish girl?"

Clown College

I WENT DOWN TO VENICE, Florida, to visit what is probably the only school in America where everybody likes the teacher and the subjects being taught. It's the college of clowns at the winter quarters of Ringling Bros. and Barnum & Bailey Circus, and the teacher, Bill Ballantine, is a former Ringling clown himself.

For my money the school was established not a moment too soon. Every winter I bring my accumulated tensions for the Ringling clowns to banish, and one thing I expect is that they will be men of outrageous energy. They must never cease to thrill to the glorious WHOMP of hitting a colleague over the head with a bladder. Yet in recent seasons they seemed to spend a lot of time just waving to the audience, or "chasing chickens," as it's known, not favorably, in the trade. What they should be chasing, of course, is each other. So why weren't they?

The incredible answer is that even circus clowns grow old. In a normal profession nobody but the boss would notice the slow and subtle loss of energy. But subtlety has no part in the life of a circus clown, nor does the luxury of aging with grace. In the end the question that must be asked is: can he still fall down? Or, more important, can he still get up?

"It was getting to a point where clowning had slowed to a walk, or really to a crawl," Ballantine told me. "You couldn't get a clown to run—he'd have a heart attack. The old spread-eagle-and-scram was gone."

The spread-eagle-and-scram is, as its name explains, the classic gesture in which a clown jumps into the air, flings his arm outward, and runs like crazy, usually to escape some form of mayhem. It's a simple—and simple-minded—motion, but one that doesn't come easily to a person who is tired, as the present Ringling clowns have good reason to be. Most of them, like the great Lou Jacobs and Otto Griebling, began long ago—and not as clowns. They were flyers who fell, or wire walkers or bareback riders who broke a leg, and they gravitated into clowning as a second career of relative serenity.

Ballantine, however, hates the very idea of serenity in a clown, and during his intensive six-week course he put his students through a physical training program that was no joke, including yoga, acrobatics, gymnastics, dance, stilt walking and elephant riding. Only at night did the school relax into mere scholarship, with the showing of films starring Laurel and Hardy, the Marx Brothers, W. C. Fields, Keaton, Chaplin and other such nobility. The dance sessions were so strenuous that one student, Leon McBryde, who had been with the Green

Berets, said: "That ballet teacher is worse than my drill instructor," which I took as a good omen. Obviously bladders will resound and prats will fall and all will be right with the world once more.

Amid the prevailing fitness one exception was Nathaniel Litt, a paunchy and sad-eyed man of thirty-seven, who, I could tell, would never make it to the top of an elephant, stilt or unicycle. Yet he brought a commitment so strong that he was changing his entire life in midstream—a thought that visits many but is entertained by few. A Manhattan architectural designer, Litt was recovering from a car accident that had killed five people, and he remembered that on his way to the hospital his main regret was that he would die without having done anything about his dream—perhaps everybody's dream—of becoming a circus clown.

"When I recovered and saw the announcement that Ringling was starting a clown college," he said, "my wife agreed that I should give it a try. 'You won't be fit to live with if you don't,' she told me." Their five-year-old son, Andrew, was less philosophical; in fact, he was downright annoyed. "Daddies don't run away to join the circus," he said. "Five-year-old boys run away to join the circus."

Litt wasn't the only middle-aged man with a good education who quit his career to attend the school. Don Ballard, forty-two, who has a master's degree in drama, was a high school teacher in Denver, and Leslie Walton, forty-one, left his job as an orthopedic technician in a Tulsa hospital. Both took with them the approval and envy of their family and friends.

Not so Jane Shirley, one of three girls in the class, who runs a dress shop with her sisters in Urbana, Illinois. "My mother cried; she said nobody would ever want to marry me if I was a clown. My relatives still don't know." Cary Patton, twenty-nine, another college graduate, who worked for the U. S. Plywood Company in Algoma, Wisconsin, also took pains not to reveal where he was going. "Only two people know about it," he said. "I told a priest and one friend. I wrote my employers and said I was going away to school. I didn't say what school."

Jan Skullerud, thirty, left a repertory company in Norway where he was an established actor playing classical roles. "I had a fantastic opportunity there," he said, "but I felt I had to get back to the *real* theater, which I think the circus is. You can use everything you've ever learned. Dance, mime, gymnastics—everything." Murray Horwitz, twenty, left Kenyon College in his senior year to attend the clown school, and when the course ended he was offered a contract with Ringling. Instead he went back to Kenyon, where he expected to graduate with a double major in English and drama. *Then* he would join the circus.

Altogether, twenty-five graduated from the clown school and fifteen—including the middle-aged architect—were given a contract, which entitled them to an eleven-month tour, at $160 a week, with one of Ringling's two units. They represented not only a new breed of clowns—bright, articulate and eager to learn—but an assault on one of the most jealously guarded preserves in show business. Ballantine remembers that none of the other clowns would speak a word to him during his entire first year with Ringling, such was their eagerness to discourage invaders on their turf.

Of all the students, only Marcos Barragon, nineteen, arrived by a traditional route. His grandfather, Marcos Droughett, is a veteran Ringling clown; his father was a flyer who fell in 1961 and was paralyzed, and his mother was a ballerina. "It's a circus family for three generations on both sides. I'm the only dropout who started late," he said. "I love clowning because I've seen the great ones—Griebling, Jacobs, my grandfather—and it hurts me to see the profession slowing down."

That answered one of my curiosities: who the students would be and what emotional credentials they would bring. But I also wanted to know about the technical details that go into a circus gag and how a comic routine gets taught.

I learned that all circus clowning is based on only six elements: blows, falls, knavery, stupidity, mimicry and surprise. Often they occur in combination. The knavery that pulls a chair out from under someone starting to sit down will result in a surefire fall. The slap delivered to one clown's face by a broom that another is carrying over his shoulder must depend on a certain stupidity in the first clown for having his face so near.

But the simplicity of the gags is deceptive. They require, first of all, perfect timing. The broom routine, for instance, is a triple gag—the second clown, being hit, turns and hits a third one with *his* broom—and it's typical of countless gags that take hours to perfect and only an instant to perform. Circus gags also must be done with exaggerated size. Ballantine kept telling his novice clowns to "open up, use your hands, use your body" and kept pulling them apart when they worked too closely. "There's so much distraction in an American circus," he said, "that everything has to be big and broad. You're working, after all, in arenas that hold sixteen thousand people. That's why clowning is hard to do on TV. It looks grotesque."

Only the element of surprise is special in the circus. If knavery is pouring water down the pants of "the victim"—and it is—surprise is when the victim shows no reaction to this indignity and then pulls from his pants a rubber bottle into which all the water has flowed. Unlike the magician, who never reveals his trick, the circus clown instantly dissolves what he has created. Typical is the "levitation gag," in which a swami seems to cause another clown, lying on a table, his body covered with a cloth, to rise into the air. At the end someone steps on the cloth (stupidity), pulling it off the levitated clown and revealing that his extended legs are really two sticks. Big laugh and everybody's happy.

But the real purpose of these revelations is a serious one: to restore everything to normal. Clowns are destroyers of order—they gratify us with their outlandish raids on all that is tidy and respectable. They do what we would like to do, but which we have been told is "not done."

Eventually, however, the disarray makes us nervous, so the clown puts everything back. There's the old gag, for instance, in which one clown performs an operation on another. Out of the patient's stomach come scarves, flowers, rabbits and so much else that the act begins to border on a domain that isn't funny. Then the patient gets up and runs off. His innards are intact, and so are the verities.

This is why clowns go to work early, doing "come-in gags" while the audience arrives. "It's mainly stuff for the kids," Ballantine explained, "so they won't be as frightened when they see the clowns later." Come-ins also used to consist, as parents remember all too well, of clowns going up into the grandstand and sitting on a woman's lap or hitting a man over the head with a hat. Ballantine wants no more of that: "It scares the kids and shakes their security—father and mother are inviolate." To say nothing of how it shakes father and mother.

Once the circus begins, come-in gags yield to "walk-around gags" and "stop gags"—quick visual jokes that fill time between the big acts. In a walk-around the clown keeps moving; in a stop gag he pauses, does his gag, and moves on, a classic example being one in which he puts a dog into a sausage machine and out comes a string of wieners. Altogether Ballantine taught his students seventy-five gags, from the small walk-around to the "big production," building wherever possible on any special talent that he found in the class.

Monty Holamon, for instance, who studied music and drama at a college in Texas, happened to be a good clarinetist, and a gag was created in which he plays a solo with great solemnity. Other clowns wander by and pause, ostensibly to admire the music, but really so that each of them can drop a half-pound weight down the back of Holamon's trousers, which, being held up by stretch suspenders, very gradually cease to be held up. Thus one of mankind's oldest sight gags is given a slight refinement.

But basically there is nothing new in clowning. Much of its appeal, in fact, lies in our recognition of so many familiar chestnuts. Proof of which was a production number called "The Doctor's Office" that Ballantine put together out of bits and pieces that clowns have begged, borrowed and stolen from each other since the earliest civilizations, or at least since the Greeks, who used clowns in their tragic dramas to break the tension.

The gag was built backward from the ability of one student, Frank Carbone, to "eat fire," or hold kerosene in his mouth, and (with Ballantine's commentary) it goes like this:

Two clowns enter, one a doctor, the other a nurse. The doctor goes to the sterilizer and takes out a hot dog, which he and the nurse eat ("that was done by Popov, the great Russian clown"). A drunk arrives ("comic drunks are as old as the Dionysian revels"), but they ignore him until he unfolds a wad of money, whereupon they eagerly bring him in to be examined ("that's the only modern touch, a comment on American medicine today").

The drunk starts to sag, so they pump him up with a bicycle pump ("a very old joke—it goes back to the bellows"), but soon he sags again. They pump him back up and put a cork in his mouth, but he sags once more. The leak must be coming from elsewhere, so the nurse takes off her falsies and puts them over his ears ("the use of falsies is classic vulgarity—you have to be vulgar with a certain finesse"). The doctor indicates that this is undignified, and he flings the falsies away, high into the air ("it's not only a funny motion; it gives the gag a new direction and takes the action off the ground—you must continually hold the attention").

The doctor puts the ends of his stethoscope into the drunk's ears to plug them, then puts the stethoscope onto the drunk's chest to listen. But he can't hear anything because the earplugs aren't in his own ears, so he runs the stethoscope across the chest of the nurse, who slaps him ("clowns are always vulgar in the sense of being earthy, or of the people, but never dirty or off color").

At this point the drunk falls out of the chair with a loud crash ("it's a punctuation point to bring the audience back—if people have missed the first part they can still catch the rest"). The doctor and nurse look down the patient's throat, but quickly reel back, and the nurse puts a clothespin on the doctor's nose ("this establishes that the drunk has a very strong breath"). The doctor points a flashlight down the drunk's throat, but it doesn't work, so he first tries tapping it on his knee and then taps the nurse on her head ("she hit him earlier"). She turns away on being hit, he turns away to get a match, and the drunk takes a swig—actually kerosene—from his flask. The doctor turns back, strikes the match and holds it close to the mouth of the patient, who blows it out, causing the "volcano"—a tremendous swoosh of flame—that ends the gag.

The whole thing, intricate as a ballet, takes only two minutes. There is a beautiful logic to it, or a beautiful illogic, whichever you prefer, and either one will do, depending on your mood. I think this is what the prophet Elijah had in mind when somebody asked him who would enter the Kingdom of Heaven and he pointed to three clowns entertaining travelers by the side of the road. Nobody offers such quick relief from the aches of the world except possibly a dentist, and the dentist isn't as much fun. My dentist's pants haven't fallen down once.

Calling All Monuments

I'VE BEEN THINKING that those big statues on Easter Island would look good if somebody bought them and put them up alongside the New Jersey Turnpike. Not only would they bring variety to a stretch of road that can get pretty dull; they would also make a wonderful tourist attraction. Surround them with burger stands and Polynesian souvenir shops, build a motor inn with a simulated grass roof, and you'd have a nice little business, not to mention a culture center. Who knows: get some kid interested in those glyphs and he might even decipher the darn things.

Best of all, it would be a real favor to Chile, one of those "good neighbor" opportunities that don't come up as often as the State Department would like. After all, the statues are in poor shape after so many centuries standing out in the Pacific wind and rain. We could fix them up with American know-how, maybe do a little restoring, and save the Chileans the trouble and expense of doing it themselves. They probably never wanted Easter Island anyway.

What started this train of thought was the purchase of London Bridge—which the English say is too narrow and frail—by the McCulloch Oil Corporation, an American firm that will take it apart and rebuild it in the Arizona desert at a resort called Lake Havasu City. Part of the Colorado River will be deflected to run under it and will be named "The Little Thames." "We believe that more than four million tourists will come each year just to see the bridge," says C. V. Wood, Jr., president of McCulloch. His company paid $2,460,000 for it, but the reconstruction cost will be lessened, according to a newspaper account, by "the fact that the bridge can be built before the river."

That, of course, is what gives the idea its integrity. For at first it might seem somewhat crude to wrench a foreign landmark out of its proper setting. But this overlooks our ability to rearrange nature with a bulldozer. I mean, it would be wrong to buy the Parthenon and rebuild it in some place that's flat—say, the outskirts of Dallas. But choose a spot that has some height anyway—perhaps across the Potomac from Washington, up by the Lee Mansion—and shape the land so it looks like the Acropolis, and put the Parthenon *there*, and the whole thing would be in such good taste that nobody could possibly complain.

Therefore I feel that we should all keep alert, as we drive around America, for suitable new sites for the antiquated monuments of Asia and Europe. The Tower of Pisa is a perfect example. It has been leaning for five hundred years, and in all that time the Italians haven't straightened it up. Obviously they're just waiting for someone to come and take it away. With our technology we could make the tower lean even more—perhaps as much as 45 degrees—and it would make a nice ornament for some middle-sized city like Bridgeport or Peoria. I say "middle-sized" because scale is so important. The Taj Mahal, for instance, is really too big for Bridgeport. I think of the Taj for Chicago, just offshore on steel piles so that Lake Michigan could serve as a reflecting pool. That's the integrity part. Without a reflection it would simply look out of place.

But technology and taste aren't the only modern American values at work here. Most exciting of all is that our philosophy of obsolescence—of disposable products, of cars that we shed annually, of buildings that we tear down after twenty years—seems to be catching on abroad. If England is willing to sell London Bridge, which dates from 1831, what chance has 906-year-old Westminster Abbey, or any landmark of Tudor or Elizabethan vintage? Soon we can expect to see Anne Hathaway's cottage at Hollywood and Vine, or Stonehenge out on Miami Beach.

And when England goes, there goes the whole ball game. Getting rid of useless historical junk will become an international sport. I can see the great hall of Karnak inside the Vehicle Assembly Building at Cape Kennedy, or Chenonceaux castle astride the Monongahela, or Hagia Sophia in Disneyland. Nor would it be a one-way project, for we have plenty of dilapidated shrines right here in the U.S.A. that national sentiment would undoubtedly like to pack off somewhere else. Just for openers, the Liberty Bell is cracked, the Capitol dome is falling apart, so is Niagara Falls, and the four Presidents on Mount Rushmore are beginning to show their age.

There's great material, in other words, for trades with other countries that would enrich both them and us. All it takes is love of culture and a little sensitivity.

Jury Duty

JURY DUTY AGAIN. I'm sitting in the "central jurors' room" of a courthouse in lower Manhattan, as I do every two years, waiting to be called for a jury, which I almost never am. It's an experience that all of us have known, in one form or another, as long as we can remember: organized solitude.

The chair that I sit in is a little island of apartness. I sit there alone, day after day, and I go out to lunch alone, a stranger in my own city. Strictly, of course, I'm not by myself. Several hundred other men and women sit on every side, as closely as in a movie theater, also waiting to be called for a jury, which they almost never are. Sometimes we break briefly into each other's lives, when we get up to stretch, offering fragments of talk to fill the emptiness. But in the end each of us is alone, withdrawn into our newspapers and our crossword puzzles and our sacred urban privacy.

The room intimidates us. It is a dreary place, done in thirties Bureaucratic, too dull to sustain more than a few minutes of mental effort. On the subconscious level, however, it exerts a strong and uncanny hold. It is the universal waiting room. It is the induction center and the clinic; it is the assembly hall and the office where forms are filled out. Thoughts come unbidden there, sneaking back from all the other moments—in the army, at camp, on the first day of school—when we were part of a crowd and therefore lonely.

The mere taking of roll call by a jury clerk will summon back the countless times when we have waited for our name to be yelled out—loud and just a little wrong. Like every person whose job is to read names aloud, the jury clerk can't read names aloud. Their shapes mystify him. They are odd and implausible names, as diverse as the countries that they came from, but surely the clerk has met them all before. *Hasn't* he? Isn't that what democracy—and the jury system—is all about? Evidently not.

We are shy enough, as we wait for our name, without the extra burden of wondering what form it will take. By now we know most of the variants that have been imposed on it by other clerks in other rooms like this, and we are ready to answer to any of them, or to some still different version. Actually we don't want to hear our name called at all in this vast public chamber. It is so private, so vulnerable. And yet we don't want to *not* hear it, for only then are we reassured of our identity, really certain that we are known, wanted, and in the right place. Dawn over Camp Upton, 1943: Weinberg, Wyzanski, Yanopoulos, Zapata, Zeccola, Zinsser . . .

I don't begin my jury day in such a retrospective state. I start with high purpose and only gradually slide into mental disarray. I am punctual, even early, and so is everybody else. We are a conscientious lot—partly because we are so surrounded by the trappings of justice, but mainly because that is what we are there to be. I've never seen such conscientious-looking people. Observing them, I'm glad that American law rests on being judged by our peers. In fact, I'd almost rather be judged by my peers than judged by a judge.

Most of us start the day by reading. Jury duty is America's gift to her citizens of a chance to catch up on "good" books, and I always bring *War and Peace*. I remember to bring it every morning and I keep it handy on my lap. The only thing I don't do is read it. There's something about the room . . . the air is heavy with imminent roll calls, too heavy for tackling a novel that will require strict attention. Besides, it's important to read the newspaper first: sharpen up the old noggin on issues of the day. I'm just settling into my paper when the clerk comes in, around ten-twenty-five, and calls the roll ("Zissner?" "Here!"). Suddenly it is 1944 and I am at an army base near Algiers, hammering tin to make a hot shower for Colonel McCloskey. That sort of thing can shoot the whole morning.

If it doesn't, the newspaper will. Only a waiting juror knows how infinite the crannies of journalism can be. I read "Arrival of Buyers," though I don't know what they want to buy and have nothing to sell. I read "Soybean Futures," though I wouldn't know a soybean even in the present. I read classified ads for jobs that I didn't know were jobs, like "keypunch operators." What keys do they punch? I mentally buy 4bdrm 1½bth splt lvl homes w/fpl overlooking Long Island Sound and dream of taking ½bath there. I read dog news and horoscopes ("bucking others could prove dangerous today") and medical columns on diseases I've never heard of, but whose symptoms I instantly feel.

It's an exhausting trip, and I emerge with eyes blurry and mind blank. I look around at my fellow jurors. Some of them are trying to work—to keep pace, pitifully, with the jobs that they left in order to come here and do nothing. They spread queer documents on their knees, full of graphs and figures, and they scribble on yellow pads. But the papers don't seem quite real to them, or quite right, removed from the tidy world of filing cabinets and secretaries, and after a while the workers put the work away again.

Around twelve-forty-five the clerk comes in to make an announcement. We stir to attention: we are needed! "Go to lunch," he says. "Be back at two." We straggle out. By now the faces of all my fellow jurors are familiar (we've been here eight days), and I keep seeing them as we poke around the narrow streets of Chinatown looking for a restaurant that isn't the one where we ate yesterday. I smile tentatively, as New Yorkers do, and they smile tentatively back, and we go our separate ways. By one-fifty-five we are seated in the jurors' room again, drowsy with Chinese food and American boredom—too drowsy, certainly, to start *War and Peace*. Luckily, we all bought the afternoon paper while we were out. Talk about remote crannies of journalism!

Perhaps we are too hesitant to talk to each other, to invite ourselves into lives that would refresh us by being different from our own. We are scrupulous about privacy—it is one of the better gifts that the city can bestow, and we don't want to spoil it for somebody else. Yet within almost every New Yorker who thinks he wants to be left alone is a person desperate for human contact. Thus we may be as guilty as the jury system of not putting our time to good use.

What we want to do most, of course, is serve on a jury. We believe in the system. Besides, was there ever so outstanding a group of jurors as we, so intelligent and fair-minded? The clerks have told us all the reasons why jurors are called in such wasteful numbers: court schedules are unpredictable; trials end unexpectedly; cases are settled at the very moment when a jury is called; prisoners plead guilty to a lesser charge rather than wait years for a trial that might prove them innocent. All this we know, and in theory it makes sense.

In practice, however, somebody's arithmetic is wrong, and one of America's richest assets is being dribbled away. There must be a better way to get through the long and tragic list of cases awaiting a solution—and, incidentally, to get through *War and Peace.*

Blondie

CHIC YOUNG has been a hero of mine for as long as I can remember. Every day for forty years he has been writing and drawing "Blondie," and every day it strikes me as not only funny but true. No matter how many solid old values go out of American life, he is one solid old value that remains.

I can't think of anybody else who enters so many lives each morning and is held in such affection. His comic strip appears in 1,638 newspapers—500 more than its nearest rival—and reaches 60 million readers. It is translated into seventeen languages, including Urdu, and has so saturated the globe that it can hardly be sold anywhere else. Proof of which is that you can get a Dagwood Sandwich in the heart of Africa.

But the language that "Blondie" speaks is, of course,

every language. We all work for Mr. Dithers, even if Mr. Dithers speaks Urdu. We all like to eat between meals and hate to see salesmen at the door. We all are a little tired. "Blondie" is a work of art constructed on fatigue. Consider this typical recent strip—typical because Dagwood is taking a nap on the sofa:

BLONDIE: Dagwood, wake up!
DAGWOOD (*awake*): Is dinner ready?
BLONDIE: You ate dinner an hour ago.
DAGWOOD: Really? I must've slept right through it.

Any writer would admire the economy of style, any artist the simplicity of line. But what really gets us is the pleasure of recognizing in Dagwood the snoozer who dwells very near the surface in ourselves, nodding, yawning, tugging at us to sneak away from whatever is boring or bothering us. Perhaps we ought to chide Dagwood for being lazy. But we don't—and we never will. His weariness reaches out to ours, and all the Protestant ethic in the world won't persuade us that his naps are sinful.

We have suffered with him, after all, through hundreds of moments when he didn't beat the system, especially in the morning. Glazed by sleep, hurtling down the stairs into clothes held out by his family, he has even kissed the mailman by mistake. That's most of us, going forth to face the day that somehow arrived too soon. If the truth has been heightened for humor, it is only by a notch. What are Dagwood's long baths but a respectable surrogate for slumber? The bathtub is one place where he thinks he can turn off the worries of the world and be left alone. That there is no such place—not even the bathtub—is the tie which binds him to that enormous bundle of fatigue called humanity.

It occurred to me, therefore, that this might be why I didn't know a single fact about Chic Young: he naps between bursts of work and never goes out of the house. I tracked him by phone, however, to Clearwater Beach, Florida, and found him awake. But I also found him jealous of his privacy and modest about having a fuss made over "Blondie" as prime American folklore. "Oh, it's just a comic strip," he said.

My hero—when I was reluctantly allowed to come see him—turned out to be a large, gentle man of sixty-nine, with sandy hair that is now mostly gone, who lives quietly with his wife of forty-two years, Athel, a former concert harpist from Rock Island, Illinois. He produces "Blondie" in a simple room at one end of the house, still the unspoiled boy who grew up in turn-of-the-century Saint Louis in a neighborhood that had "all the sound American values." He was christened Murat, for reasons which now elude him; all he can remember is that it was no name for a boy and that Chic was a welcome substitute. The family, which was of German stock, abounded with artists, one of whom, his older brother Lyman, draws "Tim Tyler's Luck" to this day.

Chic attended art classes in Chicago and launched his first comic strip, "The Affairs of Jane," in 1922. Jane's affairs interested almost nobody, so Young replaced her with "Beautiful Babs," who in turn yielded in 1924 to "Dumb Dora." Jane, Babs and Dora were all flappers, and so was their final successor, Blondie Boopadoop, whose strip was born in 1930. It is hard now to remember that the virtuous Blondie began as a gold digger trailing rich suitors, one of whom was Dagwood Bumstead, playboy son of the irascible railroad tycoon J. Bolling Bumstead. It is also hard to think of Dagwood, constant seeker of raises, as ever being rich. These two conditions, in fact, were what kept the strip from gaining momentum in the early Depression, when playboys and flappers named Boopadoop suddenly weren't funny.

At this crucial point, luckily, Young got some wise advice—that he knew more about marriage than he did about blondes. So the blonde and the playboy were married on February 13, 1933; the playboy was disowned by the Bumsteads, who vanished forever, and Dagwood went to work. "I saw that we were on the wrong tack," Young recalls, "so we just cut out all the nonsense and got in the kitchen and started talking about food and sleep, and the strip really took off."

Food and sleep are two of the four elements that have constituted "Blondie" ever since. "They're two things that everybody does," Young points out. "The third is sex, which I can't use, so I substitute raising a family, and the fourth is making money." The comic variations on these four themes have proved to be as endless in the strip as they are in life. Dagwood's efforts to earn money have their perpetual counterweight in Blondie's efforts to spend it.

"I think the reason the strip is durable is because it's simple," Young says. "I try to keep Dagwood in a world that people are used to. He never does anything as special as playing golf, and the people who come to the door are just the people that an average family has to deal with. The only regular neighbors are Herb and Tootsie Woodley; if a *new* neighbor came over with his problem, nobody would be interested."

After some 14,500 strips Young doesn't have any one favorite, but he does have favorite categories. "When

I'm stuck I fall back on Dagwood trying to get a raise from Mr. Dithers," he says. "But my real favorite is a strip that's beautifully simple." For example:

BLONDIE: Dagwood, what's that bulge in your suit?
DAGWOOD: It's my wallet.
BLONDIE: Well, it looks very bad. (*Takes some bills out.*) There, now it won't bulge so much.

"Someone might say, 'You're not going to dump *that* out in all those newspapers! It's too simple!' But it's easy to read and to look at, and the philosophy is so basic." It is indeed. In twenty-two words it compresses two truths: that a wife never thinks her husband looks quite right when he leaves the house, and that she never has quite enough money to run the house that he is leaving.

Another of his recent favorites has Blondie sorting out the contents of her purse. Dagwood says, "Why do you keep all that junk? You don't use half of it." She says, "I know—but I never know which half I'm not going to use."

A nice joke, but not such a scream that it pulls the whole strip out of shape. "I think up a lot of funny ideas that I reject because they just wouldn't be something Blondie or Dagwood would say or do," Young explains. "Boy, you stick to your characters! You don't monkey! That's something I learned from George McManus, who drew 'Bringing Up Father.' He told me, 'Don't try to be too funny every day or people will expect it. Give them just a little at a time. If you work up to a climax there's no place to go.'" As a grim example Young noted the long buildup of Andy Gump and his wife, Min, to a possible divorce, after which "The Gumps" could only slide back downhill and die.

"You also have to present nice people," Young says, "or

nobody will read the strip. The children have to be nice people. There are no mother-in-law jokes. Even Mr. Dithers has a heart of gold—he kicks Dagwood around and then says 'You're like a son to me.' Salesmen at the door are a nuisance, but I don't make them too bad—they're just doing a job. Blondie herself is never a shrew. The most I can do is make her scatterbrained. Really the only person you can make fun of today is the American Protestant husband, and even that gets me in trouble. Every strip has to make friends."

The event that first brought friends in vast numbers was the birth of Baby Dumpling, or Alexander, on April 15, 1934, and the arrival of his sister a year later was a national cause. King Features announced a one-hundred-dollar prize for the best girl's name and in three weeks got half a million letters. The winner was a Mrs. Beatrice Barken, of Cleveland, who proposed "Cookie." Where are you now, Mrs. Barken? Cookie herself, in those thirty-four years, has grown to seventeen.

"Originally she and Baby Dumpling got older in the proper sequence of time," Young recalls. "Other strips had children who were frozen at their age, and that didn't seem natural to me. So I started mine growing up. It was something new and readers liked it. But suddenly I saw that I was going to grow myself right out of a strip. So I stopped Alexander and Cookie as teen-agers.

"Still, I miss having small children around, so I bring in Elmo from down the block." Elmo keeps alive the tradition of children and dogs wandering through the bathroom where Dagwood is taking a bath—probably the biggest wedge ever driven in the national concept of privacy. Blame that on Chic Young, dads of America, as you lie soaping in full view of the neighborhood moppets.

But the survival of "Blondie" goes beyond mere adherence to sleep, food, family and money. For although these four functions haven't changed, America's attitude toward them has, and Young's most subtle feat over forty years has been to gauge the shifting tastes of his readers and to alter the strip accordingly.

"In 1930 if my readers had gone through high school they were lucky," he says. "Now most of them have gone to college. They're sophisticated and they won't tolerate humor that's out of touch. That's what killed 'Bringing Up Father.' In the 1920s and '30s George McManus had his time *perfect*. It was high entertainment—Maggie throwing plates at Jiggs. But by the '40s people no longer found husbands ducking plates funny. You had to have a truer reaction. 'Blondie' is much less physical and slapstick now. America's comic strip humor is getting more like Continental humor. People in England always thought we were a bunch of rowdies—people slipping on banana peels. Today it takes a sophisticated person to get 'Peanuts' or 'B.C.' "

"A cartoonist can get old and his ideas can get old-fashioned," Young says. "That's where I'm lucky to have Dean." Dean is the Youngs' thirty-year-old son, who now helps with the strip (they also have a daughter, Jeanne, and six grandchildren), and the relationship between father and son is a warm one. "He thinks of new situations that wouldn't occur to me," Young says, citing a strip in which a long-haired adolescent turns up at the door and Dagwood calls to Cookie that her girl friend has arrived. But it's Warren, her boy friend.

Thus Dean keeps "Blondie" responsive to the swerving currents of the mainstream. But Young is careful not to overdo it. "That's still San Francisco stuff—it's not Joplin," he says. Dean agrees: "I can usually tell what's right for

Dagwood and Blondie, and Dad says he feels it in his bones."

What Young feels in his bones, for instance, is that "when Blondie buys a dress, it's a thirty-five-dollar dress, not something you see in *Vogue*. If you want Dagwood to really hit the ceiling, make it a fifty-five-dollar dress." What he also feels is that you don't tinker with Blondie's hairdo. "I have a nondescript hairdo for her that can't be pinned down to any time or place or country." He didn't hesitate, however, to modernize Cookie recently with "a more stylish hairdo that's worn by girls her age today." Thus Cookie suddenly looks as much older as we, seeing her, suddenly feel. But that *does* happen in Joplin.

Through it all Dagwood's black suit remains constant, mainly because Young needs black for contrast in an America that has gradually paled into "decorator colors." Gone is the black stove; gone is the heavy dark furniture, and even the telephone has turned pastel.

"A comic strip is frozen to a little action of ten seconds, without sound or color," Young points out. "That's why cartoonists get to draw so well. If a fire engine comes down the street you have to hear those bells ringing." The famous spikes on Dagwood's hair were created solely to make the strip dynamic: "That hair is like the sparkle around a Christmas tree ornament. It gives the idea of things radiating from a central point and makes him look alive." As proof, Young drew Dagwood for me without the spikes and it was nobody at all.

Today Young is assisted by cartoonist Jim Raymond on inking and other details. His eyes began to fail him some years ago, and whose wouldn't? Still he remains essentially a one-man industry, which is as close as most people come to the native dream of rugged individualism. I think this is why I have so admired him across the decades. He has stuck to his vision of what is truest and best in American life and has never let us forget that humor is our saving asset.

Only in one respect does the rugged individual seem less rugged. In the 1920s Young and his wife lived in New York, and at night after seeing a show they would stop at Reuben's for one of the giant sandwiches that were a specialty of the restaurant. These later inspired him to create that even larger feat of architecture, the Dagwood Sandwich. "Dagwood is very food-conscious, so any sandwich he'd make would have to be big," Young explained.

But the explanation seemed to come from far away. "Gee," he said, "I could no more eat one of those things before going to bed *now!*"

Quenchless Me and Omphalocentric You

> In its quenchless vitality [the middle-aged generation] drinks up the golden decades like nectar at the banquet table of life. It is invisible because it defies chronology. It measures age not by a date on a calendar but by a dance of the mind.

Those were the words that I had been waiting for. Well, not *those* words exactly, but the idea that they were straining to express. In the youth-crazed journalism of modern America, awash with articles about all those finky kids under twenty-five who now outnumber the rest of us and who really run the country, here was a magazine that came right out and said something good for those of us who have turned forty. And that's not all it said.

The middle-ager can place Archimedes' lever in the exact

> spot that will shift the world a trifle closer to his heart's desire. . . . Before 40, one adds and feeds to gorge the ego; after 40, one subtracts and simplifies to slim the soul. . . . The young want to dynamite the treasure-vaults of life; middle age has learned the combination.

I mean, that's living, isn't it? Those kids think *they're* turned on? Man, we've got Archimedes' lever. They think *they've* found the nitty-gritty of life with their acidhead truths? Baby, we're inside the treasure vaults slimming the soul.

Or, rather, we were. We seem to be out again now. A mere five months after we learned the combination, it was snatched away by the same magazine. I need hardly identify the magazine as *Time*—nowhere but in a *Time* cover story do turgid generalities flower quite so richly. Besides, everyone between forty and sixty will remember this particular story. Using Lauren Bacall as its symbol ("It is this mercury of the spirit, this added luster of vitality that adorns the beauty within the beauty of Lauren Bacall"), *Time* flatly declared us to be the "Command Generation": the "top-responsibility" men and women who occupy "the seats of power" and pay the bills, the "helmsmen" who decide how the other four-fifths of America will live.

I still remember what a tonic the article was. Command Generation! Us! For weeks afterward we carried our heads a little higher, our stomachs a little flatter. We knew again what we had secretly begun to doubt: that we still *could* swim to the second float, ride that Honda, impress those nymphets on the beach with a lively dance of the mind. Oh, we were grateful to *Time* in that gilded summer and fall.

Of course it couldn't last. Soon enough the winter

frosts would chill the endocrine glands of middle-aged magazine editors and tilt the balance back to youth. But I didn't dream that it would happen so quickly, and in the same rococo prose. In fact, I had been expecting *Time's* Man of the Year to be U Thant, or at least some scientist of reasonable maturity who had harnessed the laser beam or transplanted the vital organs of a rhesus monkey.

But who did it turn out to be? That finky kid! Man of the Year! I hurried to the story inside to see what he had that we Command Generation folks suddenly didn't have:

> With his skeptical yet humanistic outlook, his disdain for fanaticism and his scorn for the spurious, the Man of the Year suggests that he will infuse the future with a new sense of morality, a transcendent and contemporary ethic that could infinitely enrich the "empty society."

Well, obviously we oldsters must have been doing something wrong. In July we were enthroned on the seats of power; by January we had built an empty society that could only be redeemed by the "Now Generation," as *Time* labeled our successors—the boys and girls under twenty-five who "have already staked out their own minisociety, a congruent culture," and who would "write finis to poverty and war." Though "psephologists call them alienated," they have a "hunger for sentience," *Time* pointed out. "In the omphalocentric process of self-construction and discovery, [the Man of the Year] stalks love like a wary hunter, but has no time or target."

Frankly, friends, that kind of writing gives me a pain in the omphalos. But it's not because I begrudge the Now Generation its swift return to the spotlight. If today's kids can write finis to poverty and war, and also infuse the future with a transcendent ethic, they should be given every chance.

What I begrudge is that there's no hiding place down here for any of us, old or young, from journalism's relentless classifiers. We are typed and stereotyped with our age bracket, and only a few tiny gaps remain for a person who would just like to be himself. The Command Generation embraces everyone from forty to sixty and merges directly into Senior Citizens. The Now Generation ends at twenty-five and reaches back to fifteen.

You might think that this leaves plenty of room in the middle—twenty-six to thirty-nine—for anyone who wants to squirm out of his assigned category. But it isn't that easy. What about the Silent Generation? I'll bet you forgot all about them. That's because they're so silent. They were silent back in the Korean war days, and they still are, but that doesn't mean they aren't *there.* They're packed solid from thirty-two to thirty-nine.

Well then, you say, that leaves twenty-six to thirty-one. Don't be so sure. How about the Beat Generation? They're in there too—right behind Silent and ahead of Now, massed in full strength at thirty-one and tapering off at twenty-seven.

That leaves twenty-six. If you want to be an individual in America today, my advice is to grab twenty-six. The only other choice is to drop back among the Teeny-Boppers, but who wants to be fourteen again? Not me. I'm having too much fun drinking up the golden decades like nectar at the banquet table of life.

The Glass Office

DISCREETLY SET among the 37 trees, 999 shrubs, 148 vines and 21,954 ground cover plants which first caught my eye when I went inside the Ford Foundation's new office building on Forty-Second Street, and which are rather hard to miss, is a small pool with 18 aquatic plants. And at the bottom of the pool are several hundred coins that have been tossed in by visitors.

Now it's one thing to carry coals to Newcastle: there always was some chance, after all, that Newcastle would run out of coals. But to throw pennies and dimes to the Ford Foundation, which has given away three billion dollars in grants and still has almost that much left in assets, would seem to be a foolish way for a person to spend his extra cash. Obviously this is not a case of logic, but of superstition, and these are not mere coins. They are offerings flung on the altar of philanthropy by those who come to ask for help.

Well might they be awed by the twelve-story temple, not only because it looks like seventeen million dollars (which it cost), but because the priests are in full view as they go about the task of dispensing similar sums. Their offices have walls of glass and are arrayed on three sides of the garden. This means that nearly everybody—including visitors—can watch nearly everybody else at work.

It is a sobering sight. True, a visitor doesn't see the 350 employees actually handing out greenbacks. But there is an air of solemnity, of noble purpose, which attends their every move, so that even the common acts of office survival—the reaching for a Kleenex, the swallowing of an aspirin—somehow seem important to the swift dispatch of aid to a school in Paraguay or a repertory troupe in Pittsburgh.

As for the gaudier acts of office survival, they are just plain out. This is no place, for instance, for a boss to make more than a verbal move toward his secretary. And it's no place to take a nap, because nobody can turn his office lights off; they all go on in the morning and they all go out at night. Even the munching of Danish pastry and the swilling of coffee from cardboard cups—traditional lubricants of American enterprise—don't seem to be traditional here.

No written or unwritten rules forbid these pleasures. It's just that the staff are on display and their environment is inhibiting. It has very little color—the carpets are all of the same pale gold, the walls of the same pale linen, the pictures from the same pale vocabulary. It's also a world where the furnishings are all alike, all quietly sumptuous (electric typewriters on brass pedestals), and all of the kind that remind their user of how tidy he is supposed to keep them. They represent the eternal dream of architects to curb the eternal sloppiness of man.

Typical is the desk that has been specially designed for the secretaries. It has built-in phones and built-in filing drawers and it looks great. The only trouble is that it doesn't work. The filing drawers open on top, depriving the secretaries of surface space, which, judging by their complaints, they need a lot more than they need a great-looking desk. Besides, the drawers filled up after only a few months.

"It's not for a working girl," one working girl told me, "but for someone who is decoration."

Everybody else has been given a desk that isn't a desk at all, but a long mahogany table which has no drawers (they attract clutter) and no telephone (it has nasty wires). It is intended to be the employee's "talk area," and I'm sure it's the handsomest talk area in town. But if the employee wants to talk on the phone, or spread his papers more messily, he must turn to his "work area," a narrow shelf behind him, against the wall, with bookshelves above and drawers below.

It is into these drawers, presumably, that all personal debris goes at the start of every day: the handbags and Hershey bars, the cough syrups and cosmetics, the *Playboys* and paperbacks. I didn't see this vital material anywhere else. A man's personality finds its main expression—if only genetically—in the photographs of his children, up on the bookshelf, smiling out from among thick reports whose titles pose all the problems of the world and a tantalizing hope of their solution. My eye yearned for a work of pop art on the wall, or for some garish trinket on the long brown tables to supplement the long brown pipe racks that are there now, full of long brown pipes. But the staff are still the servants of their new home and not its masters.

Will they strike back at the genteel designers? Will they begin to hang big calendars, put their feet up, smoke a cigar, pull down the shades and take a snooze? Will they, in short, find happiness? And will the trees and plants be "happy," clinging to life and putting forth new shoots in the air-conditioned air? Time, as they say, will tell. And what it tells could give America's office buildings an entirely different quality. For the architects have tried nothing less than to revolutionize the whole drab pattern of how white-collar workers work.

In its earlier days the Ford Foundation occupied ten floors of a building on Madison Avenue that was no more or less banal than all the other buildings on Madison Avenue. The staff communicated largely by memo and nobody knew anybody who wasn't in the same department. It was, in other words, the typical urban office with the typical urban curse—a sense of isolation within a maze of walls.

In its choice of a new site the Foundation made a gesture, first of all, to the spirit. The liberating East River was nearby. So was an entire community which shared the Foundation's concern for a better world: the United Nations, sixty-five missions to the UN, and various agencies such as the Carnegie Endowment for International Peace. Best of all, as it turned out, there was Tudor City, a complex of parks and apartments built in the 1920s in an Old English style. Suddenly this bit of period realty, long taken for granted, came into its own. With its arched windows and doors, its Gothic spires and gargoyles poking out against the sky, it provided that rarest of gifts in a city that has been progressively stripped of ornamental detail—a feeling of individuality and surprise.

To the architects who were chosen for the job—Kevin Roche and John Dinkeloo, partners of the late Eero Saarinen—it was the only graceful view available from the small and cramped site, and they oriented their plan accordingly, putting most of the offices against the north and west walls of the building so that the occupants could see Tudor City. At the same time they rejected the idea of a tower and an open plaza, so fashionable in Manhattan today, whereby an architect will set his building back from the sidewalk, raise it forty stories high, and stack as many people into it as will profitably fit. The bosses get the outside offices and the windows; the working stiffs get the "core" of the building, along with the elevators, stairs, closets and toilets.

"The people aren't considered at all," says Roche, who dislikes these buildings. "From a tower there's only one view: out. The men and women who work there don't get any community feeling—and they should. After all, they spend much of their life there. It's their other family. Everybody wants to belong and to contribute. That's when they're happiest and do their best work." Roche therefore turned the Ford building inward "to reinforce the family idea" and "make people visually aware of each other." He strengthened the family tie by giving them a private garden, and he sealed the bond of togetherness by enclosing the whole thing in glass on the sides and across the top.

The effect is rather like walking into an opulent greenhouse, except that it isn't kept at greenhouse heat. If it were, the glass would steam and nobody would see the Tudor charms of Tudor City after all. Designed by Dan

Kiley, fussed over by horticulturists, the garden brings to mid-Manhattan the varied treats of a hotter climate—exotic jacarandas and subtropical shrubs, high magnolias that will grow higher and eucalyptus trees that could reach one hundred feet, camellias and azaleas and bougainvillea vines and much more. It also has crocuses and daffodils and other flowering plants that will bloom for their brief season and be replaced on a schedule that calls for thirty changes in fifty-two weeks. And it's all at room temperature, which may be the ultimate luxury for the staff. They can keep their windows open during the day and sniff the outdoor fragrances, just as if the fragrances were outdoors.

Inevitably the garden seems not quite real, shielded behind a veil of glass from the birds and the noises beyond. But perhaps it is a herald of what our future cities will be like, for our present cities are beginning to choke on their own air, a mixture of fumes and soot that few plants will tolerate and man doesn't like much better. So it may be that our salvation lies in the experiment on East Forty-second Street. Entire blocks will be glassed over, planted with greenery and controlled by thermostat, and there, in the still and filtered atmosphere, we will reclaim our old belief that urban life is livable.

Meanwhile, back at the Ford Foundation, there's no question that Roche has achieved a community feeling. This is the real excitement of his feat in a city where almost everyone is lonely. On the first day, in fact, the staff were in partial shock. At least half of them pulled the shades down and stayed hidden, their ancient privacy intact. The next day they peeped cautiously out, saw other shades up, found friends across the court, waved, and began to relax. On the third day most of the shades went up and stayed up.

Credit for this congenial feat is given to McGeorge Bundy, president of the Foundation, who did nothing intentional to deserve it. He simply came in and went to work and gave no thought to the shades, which happened to be up. Some of the staff, however, took it as a policy decision, or at least a strong hint, and now everybody is stuck with it—Bundy most of all. Today he is the Ford Foundation's most visible asset. His tenth-floor office can be viewed by everyone walking to the two eleventh-floor restaurants and by tourists taking the guided tours. But if there is some pleasure in keeping tabs on the boss, it is a transaction that works both ways. The boss is not only seen, but all-seeing.

Other advantages continue to turn up. Fred Friendly, adviser on television, is, for instance, a man who hates to telephone somebody if that person has somebody else in his office. "People talk differently when they're not alone," he says. Now, before he calls someone like Bundy, he just takes a look to see how the boss is fixed. All these things give new zest to the working day. "It's fun," Friendly says. "It's like being on a ship. It's like walking around with a martini in your hand."

With these two similes—so far nobody *has* walked around with a martini in his hand—he expresses the staff's general satisfaction with their habitat. A few people say they feel "withdrawn" from life. When this happens they go to the north windows, which face on the street, and watch real people doing real things. But the most common criticism is of specific details which sacrifice the individual for the image, as in the case of the secretaries' desks. Happiness for the workers may finally depend, therefore, on the extent to which they can rumple the place up.

Right now it is cold. Its scale is vast, its shapes are harshly linear, the materials of its construction—granite, steel and concrete—are brutal. The garden and interiors are too self-conscious to have real warmth, and even the washrooms are done in a dark slate that seems deliberately monumental, as if to warn all who enter that this is no spot—as it is in every other office—to knock off for a few minutes and read the comics.

None of these effects, of course, is accidental. Warren Platner, who designed the interiors, says he tried to avoid "colors and materials that assert themselves." As for the pictures on the office walls, they have pushed serenity to a point just this side of sleep—an ironic turn of events for a foundation that has nourished the creative process on a scale beyond imagining. There are 364 works altogether, purchased all over the world by Andrew C. Ritchie, director of the Yale University Art Gallery, who was instructed to buy only prints, manuscripts, drawings, watercolors and maps—"and only what would be of value fifty years from now." The collection therefore has almost nothing that was done since World War II and very little by American artists. Aquatints of old Dublin and tasteful maps of the old Indies are its prevailing mood. Thus what the staff have on their walls is nowhere near as adventurous as what they have in their heads.

Nobody, however, can accuse the Ford Foundation of being timid or prissy in its larger goal—to set a fresh course for office architecture and to give New York something good. Critics say that the Foundation spent too much on its own building and should have put the money into charitable works. This is both silly and ungrateful. One of the vital roles of the Ford Foundation is to provide leadership in the formal arts and in the arts of living—a role that American capital as a whole is too indifferent or selfish to play. New York is a horror exhibit of what happens when nobody cares. The city has been turned into an architectural slum by entrepreneurs patching cheap and ugly buildings onto our daily landscape, first tearing down some structure that gave the streets their character. It is a process, week after week, that saps the spirit and glazes the mind.

The Ford Foundation building is an act of faith in the midst of ruin. Its sheer quality states the case for excellence and invites the rest of the country to aim high. As a New Yorker I'm glad to have it around. I'm glad they spent the seventeen million, and if they should ever find themselves running short I'd be happy to come over and throw some coins into the pool.

"Thank God for Nuts"

BY ANY REASONABLE STANDARD, nobody would want to look twice—or even once—at the piece of slippery elm bark from Clear Lake, Wisconsin, birthplace of pitcher Burleigh Grimes, that is on display at the National Baseball Museum and Hall of Fame in Cooperstown, New York. As the label explains, it is the kind of bark that Grimes chewed during games "to increase saliva for throwing the spitball. When wet, the ball sailed to the plate in deceptive fashion." This would seem to be one of the least interesting facts available in America today.

But baseball fans can't be judged by any reasonable standard. We are obsessed by the minutiae of the game and nagged for the rest of our lives by the memory of players we once saw play. No item is therefore too trivial which puts us back in touch with them. I am just old enough to remember Burleigh Grimes and his well-moistened pitches sailing deceptively to the plate, and when I found his bark I studied it as intently as if I had come upon the Rosetta Stone. "So *that's* how he did it," I thought, peering at the odd botanical relic. "Slippery elm! I'll be damned."

This was only one of several hundred encounters that I had with my own boyhood as I prowled through the Museum, a handsome brick building on Main Street, only a peanut bag's throw from the pasture where Abner Doubleday allegedly invented the game in 1839. Probably no other museum is so personal a pilgrimage to our past—which is saying a lot, for America has enough museums to coddle every hobby and caprice.

We have, for instance, a Museum of Whiskey History and we also have its natural enemy, a Museum of the Bible. We have museums of skiing and whaling and logging, of coins and clocks, paper and glass, rockets and trolleys and "motoring memories"—2,500 altogether, not even counting the countless roadside exhibits devoted to "petrified creatures," "the sex life of the date," and other such twilight realms of scholarship. Cooperstown alone has five, including a superb Farmer's Museum, and is something of a museum itself, its streets rich in old houses, its woods and lake rich in literary landmarks created by James Fenimore Cooper, whose father founded the town. To follow in the noiseless footsteps of Deerslayer or the Last of the Mohicans should be romance enough for any boy.

It was Cooper's bad luck, however, that a new breed of heroes came along to be enshrined in Cooperstown, and when I went there it was not in search of Chingachgook and Natty Bumppo, but Carl Hubbell and Charley Gehringer and other flanneled gods, and the only Indian I wanted to run across was "Chief" Bender, who won two hundred games in the early 1900s.

As it turned out, I could hardly go through the front door of the Baseball Museum, for it was flanked by twelve grandstand seats from the Polo Grounds, six on each side. Mere chairs, you may say: no different from any others. But there is no "mere" chair from the Polo Grounds. These were thrones for watching greatness, and anyone who sat in them was king for a day. Quite possibly I had sat in one of these very chairs myself—I spent much of my youth in that ball park and didn't consider it squandered. In any case, I sat in them again now, savoring their special hardness, lingering so long that anyone might have assumed I was studying the citizens on Main Street. Actually I was seeing Mel Ott and Bill Terry and Sal Maglie and Willie Mays.

Inside, the treasures were so profuse that it was hard to know where to turn. First homage went to a lumpy baseball that Abner Doubleday himself had evidently made, not of horsehide, and then my attention was caught by a locker. I never thought I wanted to see another locker, but this was Stan Musial's locker, brought intact from St. Louis: "The celebrated outfielder sat on the red stool changing into the uniform that hangs here."

Next I found Lou Gehrig's locker, and Joe DiMaggio's and Babe Ruth's and Walter Johnson's, each with a uniform. (Luckily, the Museum isn't such a stickler for authentic detail that it didn't first send these immortal duds to the laundry.) I found the uniform that Ted Williams wore when he hit a home run on his last time at bat: "These are the shoes that touched home plate as Ted finished his journey around the bases." Walter Johnson's shoes, by contrast, were rotted apart—as repulsive a pair as you'd see in a day's museum-going. But again there was a good explanation: "My feet must be comfortable when I'm out there a-pitching," the great man said.

Do you want to see the sliding pads that Ty Cobb wore when he stole ninety-six bases in 1915—a sight that only a mother could love, or a baseball fan? They're here. The place abounds in equipment that made history: the seat that nine Presidents sat in when they threw out the first ball, the bat that Babe Ruth used for his sixtieth home run in 1927, the bat that Bobby Thomson used for *his* home run in 1951. Even the umpires are represented; here on Olympus, at least, the men in blue are no longer hated, the rhubarbs no longer remembered. I saw the indicator, for instance, that Tom Connolly used to register the first American League pitch, in 1901, along with the gear that he wore in his last game in 1931. Who could look unmoved at such a span of service in the teeth of profanity from the dugout and derision from the stands? Or at Bill Stewart's whisk broom, worn to a nub by twenty years of dusting the plate?

I paid my respects to the Museum's famous annex, the Baseball Hall of Fame, where more than one hundred "greats" are memorialized on small bronze plaques. The room is impressive, tall as a chapel with marble columns. But it had a mortuarial air; though many of the players honored there are still living, they might as well not be, and I soon went back into the Museum, where even the dead remain very much alive, their voices audible on recordings, their signatures almost still wet on contracts and baseballs, their gloves seeming to have been put down only yesterday.

Many items would not be here—ticket stubs to memorable games, sheet music of songs like "My Old Man Is Baseball Mad"—if ordinary fans didn't send them in. No day's mail fails to bring some artifact, "like Grandpa's old glove," explained director Ken Smith. "There's a very close touch with the public." Certainly all ages were flocking through—schoolkids from the era of Koufax studying the artificial grass which is the only kind that thrives in the rainless and sunless Houston Astrodome, old men gazing backward through time at Christy Mathewson's glove or Grover Alexander's shirt. "Here's old Alex," one called to his friend, pointing to the shirt. "Here's old Eppa," the other called back, pointing to Eppa Rixey's uniform.

In the Museum's library I found its historian, Lee Allen, compiling records of the previous day's games. He had a file on every major league player and game since the first one took place in Fort Wayne, Indiana, on May 4, 1871 (the Fort Wayne Kekiongas beat Cleveland, 2–0; attendance, 200), and there was no nugget of baseball lore that wasn't within his immediate reach. If you want to know who first used a catcher's mask, the *Cincinnati Enquirer* of March 21, 1877, will tell you.

Many of the early biographical files are incomplete—a gap which Allen tried to close by visiting tombstones and town halls all over the country. Further help comes from a small legion of baseball hobbyists, one national resource that shows no sign of running dry, like the Iowa school superintendent who collects death certificates of ballplayers.

"Thank God for nuts," Allen told me, speaking as one nut to another. "That's where we get knowledge."

He had put his finger, I thought, on the real appeal of all our 2,500 museums. Big or small, popular or esoteric, they reflect our deep urge to save whatever moves us with beauty, stretches our minds, takes us beyond our daily lives, or simply entertains us. It may just be, in fact, that the collecting nuts—people who run and support museums—are the most valuable nuts around.

I dug my unspiked shoes one last time in the home plate of Ebbets Field (1913–57) and looked at the adjacent photographs of its final game, especially one that showed a woman crying when it was over and another that showed the Dodgers sitting in front of their lockers.

"Sadness is etched on the faces of the players," the caption said, unnecessarily. "None are anxious to make the first move to change into civilian clothes which will mark finis to the part they played in the Brooklyn baseball era."

Doctor Dolittle

THE LONG and highly publicized advent of *Doctor Dolittle* as a movie musical was a gloomy time for those of us who liked it as a book. Well over a year before its release the amiable doctor began to slip away from us, his round and foolish face merging into the urbane features of Rex Harrison, who had been chosen to play the title role, supported by 1,500 animals, who had been chosen to play themselves.

It was hard to miss Harrison, for instance, on the cover of *Life,* riding a giraffe, or to miss the promotion campaign proclaiming the fifteen-million-dollar film as one of the most expensive in history and heralding the Doctor Dolittle clothes, toys, books and other merchandise that would soon inundate our children. Obviously 20th Century-Fox did not share John Dolittle's cardinal belief that "money is a nuisance."

Not that all characters from children's literature are ruined by a conversion to stage or screen. The cowardly lion of Oz, thanks to one of those genetical surprises that occasionally tweak the nose of science, looked more authentic when the part was taken by Bert Lahr than if it had been taken by a lion. Other characters, like Peter Pan, simply ride out the storm. Actresses from Maud Adams to Mary Martin have, through one artifice or another, flown out a window to Never Land, but the artifice that remains strongest is Barrie's, the Peter who survives is his. E. B. White shrewdly solved the whole problem by spinning *Charlotte's Web* out of a spider, a pig and a rat.

Actually it was not on this flank that I worried about John Dolittle's defenses. He was strong enough to come out at least even in any contest with Rex Harrison. The strength of Hugh Lofting's doctor is the strength of simplicity. Perhaps no literary character since Henry Thoreau in *Walden* has been so eager to dismiss the nonessentials of life. These aren't just such obvious dismissals as giving away his money or reducing his luggage to one small bag. Sentimental clutter gets the same quick brush-off, as in the scene—redolent of a W. C. Fields movie in its baldness—where Sarah Dolittle, the doctor's sister and housekeeper, complains that there are too many animals living in the house. A crocodile that eats the linoleum is the final straw.

"If you don't send him away this minute," she says, "I'll—I'll go and get married!"

"All right," the doctor says, "go and get married. It can't be helped." And out she goes.

Surely it's one of the most remarkable replies in the literature of childhood. Yet it is unimpeachably honest. A child (or an adult) may be caught off balance, but he can't say that he has been tricked. John Dolittle is above all a direct man, and this directness would hold its own against the sly and stylish Rex.

What I did worry about was the flood of new Dolittle books that would arrive along with other tie-in merchandise. This is an area where Walt Disney sullied the whole principle of good writing for children. In the half-dozen editions of *Mary Poppins* that he published to exploit his film—editions of varying cheapness and vulgarity—there was evidently no question of using P. L. Travers' original prose, or even of mentioning her name except for copyright purposes in a type so small as to be barely visible. These books weren't written; they were nailed together by carpenters, shorn of every grace, "made simple" for moppets. Thus Disney, avid for the patronage of children, patronized them.

This was no favor to their intelligence or their integrity. Children know good writing when they see or hear it, and there is nothing accidental about the continual hold exerted on young listeners by Beatrix Potter, Frank Baum, Edward Lear, E. B. White and other authors who respect a child's right to enjoy a difficult word, even if he doesn't understand it, or to sail away on a flight of the imagination that carries no guarantee of a safe landing.

Of this small company, none so exhilarated me for pure style, when I began reading to my own children, as Hugh Lofting. Other writers may be more conspicuously elegant, more pretty or poetic. But nobody can beat Lofting for the simple beauty of a declarative sentence. His writing, like the doctor he is writing about, is strong and straightforward, wholly free of clutter. You can traverse *Doctor Dolittle* from beginning to end and not meet a passive sentence. As in all fine English writing —Shakespeare or the King James Bible, Lincoln or Thoreau, Agee or Thurber—it is the active verb that does the work and gets on with the job:

> And so, in a few years' time, every living thing for miles and miles got to know about John Dolittle, M.D. And the birds who flew to other countries in the winter told the animals in foreign lands of the wonderful doctor of Puddleby-on-the-Marsh, who could understand their talk and help them in their troubles. . . . And he was happy and liked his life very much.

It may seem simple. It isn't. The "simplified" books that movie companies generate are never as easy to read.

I don't mean, however, that Lofting's prose is all of one tone or tempo. He never hesitates to use an uncommon word that amuses him, as in the reaction of the Chief Chimpanzee to the news that in England an organ grinder's monkey is required to ask children for money: "Who would wish to live in such a land? My gracious, how paltry!"

Nor does he hesitate to play with words, to knead them into new shapes if that will suit his purpose, as in the plea of the African prince Bumpo to be taken on the voyage to Spidermonkey Island. "I am sublimely ecstasied that I did not miss you," says Bumpo, whose first year at Oxford has given him a glimpse of the English language's gaudiest regions. "Methinks I detect something of the finger of Destination in this. Even had I not gone with you, I intended at the end of this term to take a three-months' absconsion." Bumpo concludes by giving the doctor a brief report on his studies: "I liked Cicero—Yes, I think Cicero's fine—so simultaneous. By the way, they tell me his son is rowing for our college next year—charming fellow."

The last sentence is just for fun. It's pure nonsense, and all the more piquant because the author gives us no warning. Like every master of nonsense as a humor form, Lofting knows that the pleasure lies in being surprised. His books are full of such sentences, so deceptively plain that it is easy to miss the comic jewel inside: "They ran about laughing and looking over the side of the ship to see if they could see Africa yet."

But if strong active sentences are the foundation of Lofting's house, and if oddly shaped words and nonsensical loops are its gingerbread, there still remains a need for beauty—and the need is always filled when the proper moment arrives. It is then that the reader sees behind the stylist, behind the humanist who uses animals to tell us—with compassion and without sanctimony—much that is worth knowing about ourselves. What he sees is a man who has never lost his wonder at God's world.

Is there a better passage in children's literature than the one where Jip the dog, after the "conceited eagles and gossipy old porpoises" have failed to find a lost sailor with their eyes, sets out to find him with his nose?

> Then Jip went up to the front of the ship and smelt the wind; and he started muttering to himself,
>
> "Tar; Spanish onions; kerosene oil; wet raincoats; crushed laurel-leaves; rubber burning; lace-curtains being washed —No, my mistake, lace-curtains hanging out to dry; and foxes—hundreds of 'em—cubs; and—"
>
> "Can you really smell all those different things in this one wind?" asked the Doctor.
>
> "Why, of course!" said Jip. "And those are only a few of the easy smells—the strong ones. Any mongrel could smell

those with a cold in the head. Wait now, and I'll tell you some of the harder scents that are coming on this wind—a few of the dainty ones. . . ."

For a long time he said nothing. He kept as still as a stone. He hardly seemed to be breathing at all. When at last he began to speak, it sounded almost as though he were singing, sadly, in a dream.

"Bricks," he whispered very low—"old yellow bricks, crumbling with age in a garden-wall; the sweet breath of young cows standing in a mountain-stream; the lead roof of a dove-cote—or perhaps a granary—with the mid-day sun on it; black kid gloves lying in a bureau-drawer of walnut-wood; a dusty road with a horses' drinking-trough beneath the sycamores; little mushrooms bursting through the rotting leaves; and—and—and—"

"Any parsnips?" asked Gub-Gub.

"No," said Jip. "You always think of things to eat. No parsnips whatever. . . ."

Match that, you movie companies. And remember, all you moms and dads out in Kiddieland, when simplified editions of children's classics turn up in the local drugstore, borne from Hollywood on a tide of dolls and sweatshirts, there is no substitute for the best, and the idea that a child is "too young" is false economy. Sending children to a bad writer is as stupid as sending them to a bad doctor. Good doctors, like good writers, are hard to find, as the monkeys of Africa realized when John Dolittle left.

And after they had called Good-by to him again and again and again, they still stood there upon the rocks, crying bitterly and waving till the ship was out of sight.

The Map Addict

I SAT DOWN with Rand McNally's huge new International Atlas the other night, and before I knew it the fire had died out in the fireplace and dawn's first streaks were tinting the eastern sky. Actually, the fire had never been lit and my view of the east is blocked by another apartment twenty feet away, but anyway it was darn late. Which might suggest that I am a cartographer by hobby, eager to study the latest methods of rendering topographic relief or of indicating rainfall in relation to subsistence farming.

The truth is, I am just your average map nut. Look in the glove compartment of my car and you will find, stuffed inside, not a single glove. But you will find maps —road maps of states where I have never set foot, but where I can travel with my eye as contentedly as if I had grown up there. This is our addiction as a breed: we read maps the way other people eat potato chips, unable to stop. Therefore the arrival of a handsome new atlas, with 285 maps and 160,000 entries ranging from Aa (French river) to Zywiec (Polish town) is enough to put us in Nirvana (Hindu state).

Nobody knows how many of us map readers there are, for we are still a furtive lot, nursing our guilty habit in secret, reduced to sneaking a look at the Tashkent-Samarkand railway after the family has gone to bed, or plotting different ways to reach Juba or the Shan States. But I suspect that our number is growing by leaps and bounds (28 = 1 kilometer), and one of these days we will surface and do what we do right out in public, on park benches, as visible as any addict of crossword puzzles or *The Racing Form.*

Never, after all, have so many people been sent rummaging in an atlas for reasons connected with life itself and not with mere dreaming or research. Today new map readers are born with every edition of the newspaper ("Anguilla declared its independence this morning"), every postcard from a son or daughter in the Peace Corps ("he says he's in Botswana"), every visit to a travel agent ("have you thought of Sikkim?"), and suddenly the old family atlas, with its pretty old colors and tidy old balances of power, just won't work.

"What are all those pink areas, Dad?"

"That's the British Empire, son."

"The British what?"

Color, in the new Atlas, represents what God, not man, put on earth—peaks and valleys, seas and streams. Gone is green France and purple Switzerland and orange Austria, so you can no longer tell the nations at a glance. This is harder on the eyes, but easier on the sense of reality. Maybe, in fact, we can at last stop thinking of the world as a giant jigsaw puzzle and see that it is our common habitat—too good, all in all, to pollute or overpopulate or blow up.

Reality—the suggesting of round truths on a flat page—is the big achievement of Rand McNally's new book. It really *is* "international," the work of geographers in fourteen countries, its listings in four languages. But aren't all atlases international? Strictly, no. Most of them emphasize the country or area of their origin. Weren't we all brought up on atlases where Rhode Island got one page and so did China? Now the scales have been made uniform and Rhode Island looks definitely smaller.

This means that countries don't have to be preshrunk to fit on a standard page. Poor Italy, long and narrow, always used to be smaller-scaled than France, which was conveniently square. Now it takes three pages just to get from Salerno to Lake Garda, which, as any veteran of the Fifth Army will testify, is more like it. And it takes six pages to go across tiny Japan. It's like walking from New York to Omaha, give or take Jersey City.

Even the place names are for real. If Bangkok is Krung Thep to the Thai people, then it's Krung Thep—so the Atlas is obviously trying to tell us. Or, when in Roma, do as the Romans do. Not that it's always easy. Al-Qāhirah, for instance, requires more spit than the Western tongue can usually summon, which may be why we call it Cairo. Yet any tourist who has ever heard his Egyptian guide haggling with an Arab shopkeeper will agree that Al-Qāhirah has just the right mixture of consonants and catarrh. Say it aloud three times and you'll be right back in the Mousky buying a copper tray.

Getting through the cities, in fact, is what kept me up so late the other evening. For even to us map nuts there comes a moment, around midnight, when we just can't go through the Khyber Pass one more time, or poke up-river in Borneo with traders and remittance men out of Conrad and Maugham. But look! This atlas not only has the Khyber Pass stuff. It's got sixty—count 'em, sixty—maps of cities all over the world!

Thus cartography ushers us into the Urban Age, and not a moment too soon. For our hearts may be in Tahiti, but our bodies are stuck with the cities. We have become not only city dwellers but city hoppers, a vast swarm buzzing across the shrunken globe, putting down at metropolitan airports, changing our currency, seeing the required "points of interest," reconfirming our tickets, and moving on. Lisbon or Louisville, the motions are the same, the traffic as bad, the feet as tired.

Probably that's why the first thing that catches the eye on these sixty metropolitan maps is the airport, a big gray swatch as near the city as possible, but never, of course, near enough. Now the map reader can mentally land at Lagos or Djakarta, Tehran or Brazzaville, Krung Thep or Al-Qāhirah, and proceed into town past the inevitable racetrack, botanical gardens, and college of technology.

In some cities he will strike pure gold: mosques, temples, bullrings, tombs of the caliphs. Elsewhere he will stumble on colonial relics—in Singapore the airport road passes Badminton Stadium, in Bombay it skirts the Victoria and Albert Museum. But in Shanghai there is no such truck with the gentry. The palace is the Workers' Cultural Palace and the theatre is the People's Theatre.

Perhaps it is by our cities that we will finally be judged, their population having tripled in the last thirty years. If so, the map reader now joins the growing list of judges. As he combs the streets for cultural and political landmarks, he can feel at least some of the prevailing winds. In Berlin I stared with fresh disbelief at the Berlin Wall, a jagged wound in a living city. In Seoul I came upon the United Nations Military Headquarters, custodian of a fragile peace. In Detroit I found the Ford factory. In Los Angeles I found Knott's Berry Farm.

Is there a lesson in all this? Sure there is. But I'm not going to stay up looking for it. I need a good night's sleep.